MARIAH CAREY

HER STORY

CHRIS NICKSON

St. Martin's Griffin
New York

This book is for my parents,

Ray and Betty Nickson,

with all my love and gratitude,

and for **Linda**, my love, my wife.

MARIAH CAREY. Copyright © 1995 by Chris Nickson. All rights
reserved. Printed in the United States of America. No part of this
book may be used or reproduced in any manner whatsoever
without written permission except in the case of brief quotations
embodied in critical articles or reviews. For information, address
St. Martin's Press, 175 Fifth Avenue, New York, N.Y. 10010.

Library of Congress Cataloging-in-Publication Data

Nickson, Chris.
    Mariah Carey: her story / Chris Nickson.
        p.   cm.
    ISBN 0-312-13121-6
    1. Carey, Mariah.   2. Singers—United States—Biography.
    I. Title
ML420.C2555N5   1995
782.42164'092—dc20
[B]
                                                        95-9883
                                                        CIP
                                                        MN

First St. Martin's Griffin Edition: June 1995

10 9 8 7 6 5 4 3 2 1

ACKNOWLEDGMENTS

First of all, many thanks to Dave Thompson, who started the ball rolling, then kept helping with advice and answers. Jo-Ann Greene, for her pithy comments. My cheering section, for their support—Mike Murtagh, Dennis Wilken, Thom Atkinson, Kevin Odell, and Dani Byrne, Clans Hornberg, Nagel and Watkins, Lee and Greg Nickson. Madeleine Morel, for her work, and Jim Fitzgerald, for his.

Things were made much easier by the following articles: "From Big Dreams to the Big Time," by James Kindall, in *New York Newsday*; "How Sweet It Is," by Steve Dougherty, in *People*; Stephen Holden's pieces about Mariah in the *New York Times*; and Lynn Norment's article in *Ebony*, April 1994.

Last, but most certainly not least, thanks to Mariah herself for the music.

INTRODUCTION

I mean, it really is like Cinderella."
That's the way Mariah Carey described her career, in a
mixture of awe and wonder, and it really does almost seem
as if she's the heroine of a fairy tale. In a matter of a few quick
years she's gone from a poor girl, raised alone by her divorced
mother on Long Island, New York, to one of the world's leading pop divas. Her story is both inspiring and inspirational. Her
four albums have sold a total of more than 16 million copies in
this country alone. Her first five singles all reached number 1
on the *Billboard* Hot 100 chart, a feat never managed before by
anyone—not even the Beatles or Elvis Presley. Among the
many awards she's received stand two Grammys. And, as if all
that weren't quite enough, she married the man who discovered her, Tommy Mottola, the head of the company for which
she records.

"I'm really fortunate," she said. "I'm really happy, and I'm
really lucky to be where I am."

Luck certainly contributed to her remarkable success, but
in Mariah's case hard work and a huge amount of talent also
played big parts. In a business where every new act seems to
be heralded as a superstar, it takes something very special to
make an impression that lasts for more than a few months,
that continues to please the public, sell records, and to build
any kind of career. But from the moment her first album and
single were released, Mariah had that "something." *Mariah
Carey* sold 7 million copies. The four singles taken from it
spent a combined total of eleven weeks at the top of the *Billboard* charts.

For most of her life Mariah had dreamed of being a singer,

1

maybe even a star someday. Taking vocal lessons from the age of four, writing poetry since she was six, this career was something she's always worked toward. Even as a teenager, when friends would be out partying and having fun, Mariah would be busily working at her craft.

A carefully orchestrated marketing campaign by her record label, Columbia, meant that Mariah Carey was rapidly and firmly entrenched in the public consciousness. Her videos were in heavy rotation on MTV and VH-1. The Top 40 stations were playing her songs. No sooner did one slip a few spots than it seemed there was another hit climbing to take its place. The new kid in town was rapidly eclipsing the reigning diva, Whitney Houston, whose material mixed soulful ballads with hip-hop–influenced dance tunes. And it was apparent that she wasn't going to go away.

She also did something Whitney didn't: she cowrote the songs she recorded. Mariah was eager to be involved in every aspect of her music. She'd hoped to produce *Mariah Carey* herself—and did in fact produce one track, "Vanishing," as well as contributing to the vocal arrangements on several tracks.

By the time her next album, *Emotions*, appeared, Mariah was listed as coproducer and co-arranger on all the tracks, credits she's kept on all her records since then. Again, too, she wrote the lyrics for all the songs and helped write most of the music. Clearly, this was someone who would never be satisfied with just going into the studio, putting her part on tape and then going home.

Some critics have charged that things have come too easily for her, that she never paid her dues by scuffling and starving for her art. But she had no sooner graduated from high school when Mariah moved to Manhattan, taking any kind of job, however menial, that would help feed her and pay the rent while she spent her free time going from record company to record company, hoping to interest them in the tape she'd made. Even though only a year passed before she signed to Columbia Records, her dues had been paid throughout her childhood and adolescence, with constant moving, little money in the family, and the lack of a father. To most people, the dream Mariah cherished, of singing for a living, would have been simply that—a fantasy—but to her it was very, very real, and, she believed, attainable through a great deal of hard work.

Now, with her success consolidated by four multi-platinum albums, that phenomenal string of hit singles, and a short series of concerts, Mariah has well and truly arrived. She can relax at the estate she and Tommy own in upstate New York—ninety miles up the Hudson Valley from Manhattan—ride her horses, play with her dogs and cats. But almost certainly a good deal of her time will be spent learning how to make her records even better.

She remains influenced by the music she heard growing up—the soul of Aretha Franklin, Stevie Wonder, and Gladys Knight her brother and sister would play when she was a child—and by the gospel sounds she was originally exposed to when visiting her paternal grandmother and going with her to the Baptist church. Indeed, Mariah often still listens to gospel, citing Edwin Hawkins, Shirley Caesar, and the Clark Sisters as some of her favorite artists. Both these sides—and soul music itself is heavily influenced by gospel music—have frequently shown themselves in her work, from her admiring version of Aretha's "Don't Play That Song" (on *The First Vision* video collection), to "Make It Happen" from the *Emotions* album, and they seem virtually certain to remain an influence, at least in part, on Mariah's music in the future.

But she's most famous for her ballads, where she can really let fly, and use the power and range of that wonderful voice to full effect. From "I Don't Wanna Cry," off *Mariah Carey,* to *Music Box*'s "Hero," these are the songs that have really made her reputation—dramatic and emotional—following in the tradition of vocalists from Billie Holiday to Barbra Streisand to her immediate predecessor, Whitney Houston.

Musically, Mariah Carey has few worries for the future.

She can sing, she can write songs, she can produce. Her success for an indefinite time seems assured. But what about the past? Who is she? Where did she come from? How did she become such a huge star so quickly? And exactly what is it that makes her music so special?

1

P atricia Hickey was born with a wondrous gift. She could
sing—not just the way many people can, carrying a tune
or warbling in the shower, but with a rare clarity that
promised a future in music. The daughter of Irish immigrants
from County Cork, she grew up in the Midwest never knowing her father, a man who died a month before she was born.
He had been a singer himself, and a musician, and while he
could not be there to witness his little girl's growth, he was at
least able to bequeath her his talent.

At the age of seventeen her ability brought Patricia to New
York, and won her a place with the New York City Opera.
This was still a young company, organized in 1943, during
World War II, as part of the City Center of Music and Drama.
Its mission was to provide good opera at affordable prices. It
hurriedly acquired a reputation for both the quality and range
of its productions, as it began to offer premieres of new Ameri-
can works as well as revivals of classical pieces.

By 1960 Patricia Hickey had become Patricia Carey, after
meeting and marrying Alfred Roy Carey, an aeronautical engi-
neer of Afro-American and Venezuelan descent, and the couple were the parents of a son, Morgan. A year later he would
be joined by a sister, Alison. But it was a union, sadly, that
would estrange Patricia—and her children, including Mariah—
from her disapproving family.

Alfred and Patricia moved from one all-white suburb on
Long Island to another, encountering a tremendous amount of
prejudice and harassment as an interracial couple, a pairing
that was not so common in those days, and one which tended
to generate extreme reactions. "They went through some very

hard times before I was born," Mariah told *People* magazine. "They had their dogs poisoned, their cars set on fire and blown up." Not unnaturally, these events caused many problems. "It put a strain on their relationship. There was always this tension. They just fought all the time."

But by the late sixties, Patricia was at last achieving some success in the operatic world. Still with the New York City Opera, the mezzo-soprano had become a soloist in the company, working with such world-famous names as Beverly Sills.

Then, in the fall of 1969, Patricia discovered she was pregnant again. And on March 22, 1970, Mariah Carey was born.

The world she entered was a violent place. Fighting was going on in the Middle East. The conflict in Vietnam continued, claiming thousands of lives—indeed, a week after Mariah's birth, a war protest at Kent State University in Ohio would result in the deaths of four students, shot by the Ohio National Guard. But at the same time, ironically, Simon and Garfunkel's gentle, hopeful "Bridge Over Troubled Water" was number 1 on the *Billboard* Hot 100, enjoying a six-week run in that position.

Although Mariah once jokingly stated, "I think my mother chose the name Mariah because it would be a good stage name," Patricia actually took the name from the song, "They Call the Wind Mariah," featured in the Lerner & Lowe musical *Paint Your Wagon,* which, as a film, was enjoying great popularity in 1970. (A song from the movie, "Wand'rin Star," sung by Lee Marvin, was number 1 in England the day Mariah was born.)

Mariah was a good deal younger than Morgan, who was ten at the time of her birth, and Alison, who was nine. The family, sadly, continued to be the target of rampant racial intolerance, and the ongoing problems it caused in the relationship between Alfred and Patricia proved insurmountable, causing their separation and divorce, which occurred when Mariah was three. Alison went to live with her father, while Morgan, just in his teens, and Mariah stayed with Patricia. At first they saw their father weekly, but those visits soon became less frequent, although still amicable. "My father and I had a good relationship for a minute there, right after the divorce," Mariah recalled. "Everybody wishes they had a 'Brady Bunch' family, but it's not reality.

"He's a good person," she elaborated. "I don't have anything against him. It's just very difficult growing up in a divorced family—the tension, anger and bitterness between the parents is often put off on the children, and because I was so young when they divorced, it was a *major* split for me." She discovered, in her visits with her father, that they really had very little in common. His talents as a mathematician weren't passed on to his younger daughter, and he didn't share her love of music. However, Mariah did retain some fond memories of the time they spent together when she was young. Alfred Carey eventually took a job in Washington, D.C., and moved there, but continued also to maintain a home on Long Island.

For all the problems, the conflicts, and arguments between them, Patricia never tried to turn the children against their father. Mariah recounted, ". . . [L]ucky for me, my mother never said anything negative about my father. She never discouraged me from having a good feeling about him. She always taught me to believe in myself, to love all the things I am. In that sense I'm very lucky, because I could have been a very screwed-up person."

By the time of the divorce, though, Patricia had discovered that her younger daughter had inherited her singing talent. It happened in 1972, as Patricia was rehearsing at home for her debut as Maddalena in Verdi's opera, *Rigoletto*.

"I missed my cue," she explained once, "but Mariah didn't. She sang it—in Italian—at exactly the right point. She wasn't yet three."

Once Mariah had found that she possessed this ability, she used it constantly. She walked around the house "like a little tape recorder, and I'd mimic whatever I heard, whether it was my brother's or sister's records, or whatever songs were on the radio at the time." What she heard mostly, though, was her mother's voice. Patricia was still with the New York City Opera, and would often rehearse her roles at home. Little Mariah would sit next to her, correct her errors in pitch, and sing along—in Italian, her mother told her years later, although Mariah was unable to remember it. So Patricia was definitely the person most responsible for exposing Mariah to music from the time she was an infant.

And music *was* always around the house. The newly single Patricia had a difficult time making ends meet. Her position at the Opera didn't offer enough money, forcing her to become a freelance vocal coach. She happily encouraged Mariah's musical precociousness. "I grew up on my own with my mom," Mariah said. "I was always singing around the house because *she* was always singing, so I would try to mimic her. She couldn't shut me up. She wouldn't let anybody baby-talk around me. She had me around all her friends as a kid, and she used to say I was like a little adult. All I wanted to do was sing for my mom's friends, so I would memorize every jingle on TV, and whatever records were playing around the house, like Stevie Wonder, Aretha Franklin."

Once Mariah was four, although she considered her "a born singer," her mother started giving her voice lessons; the raw ability was obviously there, but she needed training to learn how to use and develop it properly, and only formal study would give her that. This shared talent and time reinforced the bond between them, in a family that was always financially on the brink. "I grew up without having a lot of things, money and stuff like that. My mother and I moved around a lot; she worked three jobs sometimes. I went through a lot of rough times when I was a little girl." A lack of money creates constant strain and strife, and a vicious cycle of near poverty—most certainly a sense of living on the edge. Everything that comes into the house immediately goes out again to cover bills; there's no chance to save, to get ahead, no sense of security, just a feeling of always struggling.

And they did struggle. Over the course of fourteen years, Patricia and Mariah would move thirteen times in the New York area as Patricia sought work in her field. But she was always there for her daughter, encouraging and supporting her. It's her mother, Mariah said, "who is most responsible for me having the courage to be able to do what I'm doing." Patricia took great pains to instill a strong, healthy sense of self-esteem in her daughter, and to reinforce the idea of the girl's talent. It was a spark, Mariah was certain, that gave her the strength to become a professional singer.

Patricia's work wasn't limited to daytime hours. Singers often perform long into the night, and vocal coaches frequently work in the evenings. Whenever possible, she would take Mariah with her, but frequently that wouldn't be possible. "My mom and I almost grew up together," Mariah said. Being together so much made them almost seem like a team, and being around adults caused Mariah to grow up quickly—a trait that was extremely useful on those occasions when her mother had to work at night and Mariah had to stay home alone, with only the radio as a baby-sitter.

It was during this time that Mariah Carey made her real singing debut. As a first grader, she was co-opted for a high school production of the musical South Pacific, in which she soloed on the tune "Honey Bun."

Her musical education was continuing, too, in more ways than one. Patricia's friends would visit, and everything from the late jazz singer Billie Holiday to opera would be played. Mariah was also encouraged to take piano lessons to complement the voice training, but, by her own admission, she was "lazy"; it's something she now regrets. "When I was little, my mom tried to get me to do piano, but I said, 'This comes naturally, I can do it by ear. I don't want to learn.' I should have taken lessons because it would be easier for me now. . . . Sometimes ideas just come, and because I'm worrying about trying to find the chords, I end up losing part of the idea."

Then there was also the soul music that Morgan and Alison loved, that Mariah had mimicked as an infant, and then grew to enjoy herself, and which would eventually lead her to one of the great, ongoing loves of her life—gospel music.

So many of the soul singers that Morgan and Alison listened to had grown up singing in the Baptist church—Al Green, Aretha Franklin (whose father was a famous preacher), Stevie Wonder, Gladys Knight—and it showed in the way they approached their music. Once Mariah discovered that two of her idols, Al Green and Aretha Franklin, had both recorded gospel albums, she went out and bought them.

It proved to be a major turning point for her, and very soon she was investigating other gospel artists who hadn't made any secular records, people like Shirley Caesar, the Clark Sisters, Mahalia Jackson, and Vanessa Bell Armstrong. The rawness and freedom of the voices touched a chord in the girl, one that would continue to resonate inside her, to influence and motivate her. She has stated that even now she prefers to listen to gospel over both pop and R&B, and has admitted buying gospel tapes from late-night television. And it has frequently shown up in her music, whether it be in the soaring arrangement of the backing vocals, or the way a piano is played, or the rich tones of her own voice.

But her introduction to this music had come on the sporadic visits she made to her father's mother, whom Mariah would accompany to the Baptist church where she would hear traditional spirituals. These times were the only instances during her childhood that Mariah was able to experience the sensation of being part of a large family. Unfortunately, the visits were rare. "I wish I had been part of it more," she said.

MARIAH NEVER HAD any choice but to be well aware of her racial background. It was something that definitely added to the problems she felt as a child. "It's been difficult for me," she explained in an interview with *Ebony*, "moving around so much, having to grow up by myself . . . my parents divorced. And I always felt kind of different from everyone else in my neighborhoods. I was a different person ethnically. And sometimes that can be a problem. If you look a certain way everybody goes, 'White girl,' and I'd go, 'No, that's not what I am.' " But while the brief time she had spent with her grandmother had served to make her very aware of her black heritage, she knew she wasn't completely black, either. She felt it upset people that she refused to come out and state she was one or the other. However, it was impossible to do without denying a big part of herself. To call herself black would ignore her completely Irish mother ("my best friend"). At the same time, saying she was black, Venezuelan, and Irish satisfied no one; it appeared to be too much of a compromise. For Mariah, though, it was all she could do, because it was the truth, and it brought home to her the ultimate difficulty in being an interracial child—being neither one thing nor the other. So she defined herself in the only possible way—"I am a human being, a person."

All three of the children found themselves on the receiving end of prejudice. Alison had the darkest skin in the family, and the neighborhood kids would single her out. "They'd shout racial slurs and beat her up," Mariah recalled with a mixture of sadness and anger. "Then my brother would go in and fight for her, even though he was handicapped. [Morgan suffered from cerebral palsy and epilepsy.] It was tough."

And when she was down and gloomy, Mariah could always disappear into her music. Where other kids might stand in the driveway and shoot endless baskets, she would walk alone in the woods, or anywhere she could be by herself, and let her voice ring.

Mariah was also finding another way of expressing herself—writing poetry, although it didn't always go over well in class. In a manner that's unfortunately all too common in schools, when she handed in her poetry assignment, her third-grade teacher, Mr. Cohen, refused to believe that she could have done the work herself, and accused her of copying the lines from a book.

But at home there would always be that best friend, her mother, "the mainstay in my life," ready with all the comfort and support she could muster.

IN THE VERY BEST of circumstances, where both money and time are no problem, being a single parent is a difficult task. Patricia Carey's circumstances were far from ideal. Like most single mothers, she had to work to support herself and her daughter. A great deal has been written about the plight of single parents, and the wide range of financial and emotional problems they and their children face.

When a family breaks up, the initial impact is, of course, bound to be economic. A U.S. Census Bureau study, conducted in 1984, showed that at that time the average family income in the New York City metropolitan area was $2,435 per month. One month after a father left the family, that figure took a sharp dive to $1,543. After six months the amount had rebounded slightly, to $1,711 per month, but the difference of $700 a month was still a great deal less than when both parents were present—which translates into trouble in both the short and long term.

The problem is compounded by the fact that women, as a group, make less money than men. For single mothers, that rings especially true. A 1988 Census Bureau report found that the average single male parent's income was $38,339 a year. For a woman it was $22,343. When housing, food, utilities, clothes, and all the other factors are included, this extreme disparity places single mothers in a precarious financial position, particularly those who are dependent on a separated or divorced husband to contribute child support on a regular basis in order to make ends meet. Ninety-four percent of all child support paid in this country is by men to women, and far too many males—more than 20 percent—fail to fulfill those court-ordered obligations to their families, leaving their ex-wives no option but to seek work, often at any level they can find, which translates financially into minimum-wage positions, which forces them to be away from the home when they need to be there for the children. Today, 11 percent of all children are "latchkey kids"—that is, they return from school to an empty house. For those under the age of ten, the figure is 8 percent, more in the cities and suburbs than the rural areas, which can have a damaging long-term psychological effect on the youngster.

That damage frequently also extends to the mother's psychological position. The Department of Sociology at Iowa State University, which studied 209 divorced women, concluded that single mothers face a greater risk of psychological problems and ineffective parenting than married women, and that the major cause of this was economic uncertainty and the stress it caused.

In 1992 there were 13.7 million children, or 22 percent of the entire under-eighteen population in the United States living with a single female parent—an immense figure! This stood as a huge increase over 1960, when the figure was 8 percent. A total of *one-third of all mothers* were raising children without their spouses. So Patricia and Mariah were far from alone in their situation. However, since Patricia Carey didn't have a "regular" job, with a set salary that at least allowed for some planning and budgeting, working instead as a freelance vocal coach, never knowing exactly how much she'd earn each month, her stress level must have been very high. So, quite understandably they didn't have much money while Mariah was growing up, as she has said; but, a friend told *New York Newsday*, "She never griped about it."

The closeness between herself and her mother that Mariah has often talked about turns out to be quite common among daughters raised by single mothers. In those situations, according to some psychologists, mothers tend to have a particularly heavy influence on their daughters, due in no small part to the amount of time necessarily spent together. Now, that can also be true in families where the father is present, too, but it becomes especially notable when girls are raised solely by the mother. As the old proverb goes, "A son is a son till he takes him a wife, but a daughter is a daughter for the rest of her life. . . ."

Like Patricia, many women have made a successful job of raising children on their own, and it's true that the vast majority of kids grow up to be fine, productive adults. But being a single parent definitely does make the task more difficult; a Canadian study, conducted in 1981, showed that the children in such families were more prone to aggressive and antisocial behavior—from school disturbances to criminal arrest—by a margin of 6 percent to 27 percent. Those figures make some sense; a single mother, struggling to survive, has less time to spend with her offspring, and in that limited time she has to try and be both mother *and* father, a virtually impossible task. No study has been attempted to show links between single-parent families and attempted or actual juvenile suicide. But when national surveys of school-age children indicate that 11 percent of boys and 8 percent of girls have made at least one attempt at suicide, it would appear that there is probably some connection, if only by sheer numbers.

Almost half of the children of single mothers (48 percent) are in day care of some kind while their mothers work. But when a child is sick, the parent has to leave her job, sometimes for several days, to nurse and care for her baby. This time away creates a multitude of problems. The biggest, obviously, is a loss of wages. And that doesn't necessarily just mean for hours absent from the workplace; in 1987, 6 percent of all working women lost their jobs or had their hours reduced because of time lost from the job due to absences related to their children.

The crisis of single mothers is often thought of (and reported) as one that has its greatest impact on minorities—and while it's certainly true that the black community does have 3 million of them, the vast majority living in urban areas— when the dilemma is looked at throughout the country it crosses all racial boundaries. In New York City, 30 percent of all Caucasian mothers are single. For African-Americans, that figure is 40 percent, and for Hispanics 20 percent. Financially, white women have a slight advantage over minorities, and those in the suburbs have a greater income than those in urban or rural environments. But the fact is that no one enjoys a privileged position; it's hard times all around.

What all these figures show is that the greatest challenge facing one-parent families, of any color, is to establish some kind of economic stability and security. When income and expenses barely meet, it's impossible to establish any kind of savings and be prepared for the emergencies that inevitably arise. So, when they do, the family plunges into debt, creating a cycle of poverty from which it's difficult to escape.

But, after several long years of constantly struggling and moving, the Careys managed to establish a place of their own. Finally, when Mariah was a teenager, she and her mother were able to settle in one place for longer than a few months. On Long Island, they had an unassuming house in an affluent neighborhood of Huntington Bay, which, an unnamed friend said, "might have been tough on her,"—a reference to their monetary situation. "I never had any financial security," Mariah said, recalling her childhood. "I dreamed of possessing things. Lucky for me I had my music to hold on to as a goal. It was like, 'These people may not think I'm as good as them, but I can *sing!*' "

By the time Mariah entered Greenlawn's Harborfields High School, she was already writing songs, something she'd begun in junior high, and by the age of fourteen she already had an after-school job as a singer on demonstration records at a few local Long Island studios. These were her very first steps towards realizing her dream of singing and writing music for a living. As her school friend Patricia Johnson told *New York*

Newsday, Mariah knew from the time she was in seventh grade exactly what she wanted to do with her life. "And she always did what she said she was going to do."

Patricia was still giving her daughter vocal training, working to bring to fruition the talent Mariah had shown as a little girl. She was careful, though, not to impose the values of her own classical training on her daughter. ". . . [She's] never been a pushy mom. She never said, 'Give it more of an operatic feel.' I respect opera like crazy but it didn't influence me." Indeed, although she knew and greatly admired the technical ability involved in opera, the music never touched her, and she had no desire to subject herself to the endless years of training necessary to become a diva or a prima donna.

At Harborfields High Mariah didn't publicly display her ability. Quite deliberately she didn't join any of the school choirs or take part in any talent shows. Her music was still a very private, personal thing, and that was the way she wished to keep it. But otherwise she was a perfectly normal student—outgoing, popular, and full of self-confidence, which earned her the nickname "Miss Mod."

"I'd hang out with my friends," she reminisced, "and go to parties, and just be stupid and goof off, but when I was at home, I was listening to music and writing songs." And in comparing her conversation with her friends, her focus becomes quite evident: "Girls growing up talk constantly about having babies. I talked about music."

By now she had a writing partner, a friend, Gavin Christopher, and the songs they were producing so impressed Morgan Carey that for his little sister's sixteenth birthday he paid for her to make her own demo tape in a professional 24-track studio in Manhattan. "We needed someone to play keyboards for a song. . . ." Mariah explained to Fred Bronson in the *Billboard Book of Number One Hits*. "We called someone and he couldn't come, so by accident we stumbled upon Ben [Margulies]. Ben came to the session, and he can't really play keyboards very well—he's really more of a drummer—but after that day, we kept in touch, and we sort of clicked as writers."

That line is a great understatement; the pair would go on to achieve the incredible success of the *Mariah Carey* album. But that time was still a long way off. For now they would have to be content with perfecting their craft, writing songs and laying the groundwork for the future.

Ben's father owned a cabinet factory, Bedworks, in the Chelsea area of Manhattan, and he'd allowed his son to set up a studio in a back room there. So it was to Bedworks that Mariah began commuting—with her mother's permission—on a regular basis, often staying out until two in the morning. Trying to juggle school, music, and sleep, it was inevitable that something would suffer. So it was perhaps no big surprise that around this time her nickname changed to "Mirage," indicating her frequent absences from school.

The duo quickly began completing material. The first song they wrote and recorded together was called "Here We Go Round Again." It was a tune with a great deal of Motown influence; Ben creating the music, Mariah writing the lyrics. As they listened to the completed tape in the tiny studio behind the woodshop, the excitement grew. It didn't just sound good—it sounded *incredible*! And so a partnership was born.

But still Mariah kept quiet about her ambitions at school, at least until she was called upon to explain why her schoolwork was so mediocre. Then, assistant vice principal John Garvey explained, "When you talked to her about it, she'd let you know it just wasn't that important in her life because she was going to be a rock star. She was fully convinced it was going to happen. Nothing was going to stand in her way. You could talk to her until you were blue in the face and it didn't do any good."

Mariah didn't view things in quite the same way. To her, all that this nagging meant was a lack of support for her dream. The teachers picked on her because she didn't want to follow the conventional track. She had no desire to pass math and get into a good college—or any college, for that matter. She didn't need it. It didn't matter. She was going to be a singer.

One person who did offer her some support was her high school counselor, James Malone. He encouraged her to follow her dreams, but suggested that she develop other skills, in case, like so many, her dreams never came true. He even told her that if singing didn't work out for her, she was always welcome to return to him, and he'd offer whatever advice he could on a career path. "You know," he mused in 1991, "I don't think she's going to need that counseling now."

No matter how concentrated Mariah was on singing, though, in at least one area the teenager in her shone through—her room was always messy. And, of course, Patricia would wonder how she'd manage when she was eventually living alone and had to clean up after herself. "Well, I'm going to be a famous singer and have a maid," was Mariah's half-joking response.

Besides working hard to support her family, Patricia had not put her personal life entirely on hold throughout this time. She'd met a man, Joseph Vian, fallen in love, and while Mariah was in her senior year of high school, the two married. Sadly, it wasn't destined to last; the divorce between the couple became final in 1992.

Perhaps to the astonishment of a few of the teachers who'd found her attitude toward classes incomprehensible, Mariah graduated from Harborfields High School with the Class of '87. In her senior yearbook she listed her likes as "sleeping late" (not too surprising, all things considered), "Corvettes," and "guiedos" (sic)—Italian men.

Then, within a few days, as if it couldn't happen fast enough, she'd packed all her stuffed animals, her posters, tapes, and clothes into boxes, and she'd moved to Manhattan. Mariah was looking for the Big Time.

2

So, at seventeen (the same age her mother had been when she moved there) Mariah was living in New York City, trying everything she could think of to make her dream come true. She had a place to live, a one-bedroom apartment she shared with two other girls who also aspired to be performers. It was, to say the least, a cramped existence. Mariah slept on a mattress on the floor of the living room. None of them had any money for more than the basic necessities, to the point that sometimes eating would get classed as a luxury. More than once the roommates stretched out a boxed macaroni-and-cheese dinner over the course of a week.

All Mariah's free time was spent pursuing her musical goal. She went, on foot, to virtually every record company in town, carrying the demo tape she and Ben had made. But, as she explained in an interview with the *Chicago Tribune,* "For . . . a year I couldn't pay someone to listen to my tapes. They think if you don't have a high-powered manager or don't have a record company that's already interested in you, you're no good. I had no connections and I was running with my writing partner, who was also new and didn't have any connections, either."

It was a very frustrating situation, one encountered by any number of new artists. All they have to keep themselves going is their music and a large amount of faith. Ben's studio didn't even have more than basic equipment. But he was sure their demos sounded good. And he never had any doubts about Mariah's exceptional talent, as he was happy to tell: "She had the ability just to hear things in the air and to start developing songs out of them. Often I would sit down and start playing

something, and from the feel of a chord, she would start singing melody lines and coming up with a concept."

But, apart from the time spent recording at Bedworks with
Ben, or trying to get a foot in the door with a record company,
Mariah also had to earn a living. To do that, she held a series of
jobs, most of which she lost because she had "an attitude." It
was all work of the "easy come, easy go" variety. She hat-
checked in clubs, hostessed and waitressed at restaurants like
the Sports Bar and the Boathouse Cafe in Central Park. But
none of it paid her a living wage. She owned one pair of sneakers, full of holes, that she had to wear every day, even during
winter's worst wet slush and snow. Then, at home, if they
were lucky, there was a single plate of pasta to split between
the three girls.

Mariah didn't care in the least about these jobs; they
weren't her future. Music was her obsession. Even at work it
filled her mind. "I'd be sitting there watching some video—
Debbie Gibson or something—and I'd be fuming furiously.
Like 'Why do I have to sit here and waitress while these people
are doing videos?' "

At least she used some of this time productively. All too
often she'd be discovered, after much fruitless searching and
yelling, sitting with a pair of headphones cutting off the outside world, singing along to a tune and working on a set of
lyrics for a new song, when she should have been looking after
customers. And, almost invariably, that would mean the end
of another job.

Out of this awful procession of labor, there was one position that stuck in her mind as being without question the *very*
worst. For two days she swept up the cut hair in a salon owned
by a man who liked to give his employees names like "Light-
ning" and "Electricity," which would be displayed on plaques
above their stations. While this struck Mariah as strange, she
didn't pay it too much mind until the owner—after repeatedly
staring at her and asking her name—announced that from that
point on she would be known as "Echo." When she asked

why, he explained that when someone worked in his salon, he named them. Needless to say, that didn't sit well with Mariah. In fact she quit on the spot. There was always another job, and it had to be better than *that.*

Being young, she could push herself to the limit, and she did. Every day she worked, waitressing—or whatever her job was that week—until midnight. As soon as her shift was over she'd join Ben at Bedworks and work until 7 A.M., when she'd go home and sleep until it was time to get up for work again. Almost her only break from the routine came when she'd make the round of record companies again.

But there was never any doubt in Mariah's mind as to why she was putting herself through such misery—she was certain of what the future would hold: "I was doing all that because I wanted to get a record deal and make an album. I can do things that aren't productive or I can make an album."

After several months of these menial jobs, things did begin to look up. Mariah had become friendly with a number of musicians, one of whom played drums for an R&B singer named Brenda K. Starr. He mentioned that one of Brenda's backup singers had recently quit, and suggested to Mariah that she apply for the job. "I really didn't want to do it," she told Fred Bronson, "but I said it's gotta be better than what I'm doing now. So I went to the audition, and Brenda was such a great person."

The range and fluidity of Mariah's voice impressed her prospective employer, and suddenly she was realizing a little bit of her dream—she was making some of her living from singing. Unfortunately it was only a part-time gig; Brenda wasn't a big star, so she couldn't keep musicians and singers on the payroll full time. But it was a start.

This new job didn't do much to improve Mariah's finances. She still had to wear the same holey sneakers she used for work and walking across town, and she always seemed to be dressed in a single outfit that consisted of a short jacket and a pair of black stretch pants, no matter how bitter the New

York winter weather. In fact, it reached the point where Starr began to worry about the health of her new backup singer, that she might end up catching pneumonia in such thin clothes.

Brenda had a record contract with CBS Epic (for whose big-sister label Columbia Mariah would soon be recording herself), which at this stage put her ahead of Mariah. She would release an album, *Brenda K. Starr,* on MCA, and *By Heart* on Epic in 1991, as well as contributing to three soundtracks: *License to Drive, She's Out of Control,* and *George LaMond: Bad of the Heart.* Although Mariah never recorded as a part of Brenda's band, she did take part in a number of live shows with her, and over the course of their time together the two became good friends. Sometimes, when there were no gigs scheduled, and Mariah wasn't working on her own material, the two would spend an evening sharing and chatting. Neither had grown up with a father, and it was a subject that still rankled them both.

The friendship between the two grew quickly, by leaps and bounds, and Brenda recognized and happily acknowledged Mariah's unique talent. "Most singers would have said, 'Stay in the background and don't sing too loud,' " Mariah told *People.* Instead, Brenda began promoting her discovery, introducing Mariah to the contacts Brenda had in the music industry. A few years later Mariah had nothing but praise for her friend and former boss: ". . . She helped me out a lot. She was always, 'Here's my friend Mariah, here's her tape; she sings, writes . . .' "

And, once Mariah had achieved her success, she never forgot Brenda. At one time Starr was going through a bad spell. She was living in New Jersey, trying to get by on very little money. Christmas was coming, and things looked bleak. Out of the blue, completely unannounced, Mariah arrived, bringing a rocking horse from F.A.O. Schwarz for Brenda's daughter, and an extremely expensive makeup kit for Brenda herself.

"She started laughing with her curls falling in her face," is the way Starr happily described the scene. "It was like she was Santa Claus. I started crying."

But perhaps such gifts were only appropriate. After all, if it hadn't been for the persuasiveness of Brenda K. Starr, Mariah might have ended up waiting a lot longer for her recording contract. . . .

TOMMY MOTTOLA had become head of CBS Columbia's U.S. organization in the spring of 1988, replacing Al Teller not long after Sony's takeover of the industry giant. It was one of the senior jobs with what was still the country's biggest record company, an extremely powerful position. A genial, bearded man, he had charge of an operation that was doing well, with top-selling, established artists like Billy Joel and Barbra Streisand. However, there were problems. A competitor, Warner Bros., was rapidly increasing its share of the market, and Columbia didn't have many new acts that it could break and make money. Making those changes had to be Mottola's priority.

Born in 1952 in the Bronx, Tommy Mottola had been involved with music all his life. He studied acting and voice at Hofstra University, on Long Island, and while there managed to win a recording contract with Epic (ironically one of the Columbia labels), where, under the name T. D. Valentine, he released several singles, including "Love Trap" and "A Woman Without Love." None became a hit. So, with a degree, but having been dropped by the label, Mottola moved to the business side of the music industry, starting out as a promotion man for the large music-publishing company, Chappell Music. In his early days there he came across Hall and Oates, at the time a struggling young band, and eventually helped them find a record deal on Atlantic (after Epic had turned them down). Then, in 1975, he founded Champion Entertainment with Sandy Linzer, a former Epic staff producer, and began managing not only Hall and Oates, but also Odyssey and Dr. Buzzard's Original Savannah Band. A few years later Champion would be handling the careers of such stars as John Mellencamp, Split Enz, and Carly Simon, and Hall and Oates would write about him on their *Silver* album in the song "Gino (The Manager)."

Married with two children, the move to Columbia was a definite step up the business ladder for Mottola, and some expressed doubts as to his fitness for the job. But he was well aware of his priorities, that Columbia had no female star to challenge Whitney Houston (who recorded for Arista) or Madonna (whose records appeared on Sire). He wanted to find a pop diva for Columbia. And quickly. It could solve all the problems.

SO EXACTLY WHAT—and who—is a pop diva?

The pop diva—a female superstar who can sell millions of records, whether they're ballads or uptempo tunes—has been an increasing factor in the music business since Barbra Streisand. Some might even say it goes back further, to Judy Garland, a troubled woman who could invest a song with total, believable emotion. But Streisand was the point at which "recording star" became truly a "superstar."

Barbara Joan Streisand was born April 24, 1942, a full generation before Mariah, in Brooklyn, New York. By her own admission, she regarded herself primarily as "an actress who sings" rather than a singer, and took part in several theatrical productions before turning to singing as a way to support herself between acting jobs (at the same time changing the spelling of her first name to Barbra, "to be different"). But an initial two-week engagement at Bonsoir, the Greenwich Village club where she won a talent contest, was extended to eleven weeks, and then she moved to another, larger club, the Blue Angel. Word of her particular magic circulated quickly and soon she was back in the theater—this time as a star of musicals. Her first role was that of Miss Marmelstein in *I Can Get It for You Wholesale,* and, following rave reviews for that role came her breakthrough part: playing Fanny Brice, the lead in *Funny Girl,* on Broadway; then, in an unprecedented flurry of publicity, in London.

Suddenly a huge international star, the albums she released—which tended to feature older songs rather than contemporary material—rocketed to number 1. However, she continued to act as well, finding time for movies, recording, and Vegas shows, and demonstrating the Midas touch with everything she turned her hand to. Over the course of her career she's recorded five number 1 singles ("The Way We Were," "Evergreen (Love Theme from *A Star Is Born*)," "You Don't Bring Me Flowers," "No More Tears (Enough Is Enough)," and "Woman In Love"), and has moved with the greatest musical ease through every field, from cabaret to show tunes, to rock and even disco.

Retired for many years from performing, her comeback concerts in the U.S. and England literally sold out in under an hour at the start of 1994. There's absolutely no doubt that she has set the standard, not just for female singers of her time, but for every female star that has followed. Her perfectionism is legend (and the cause of many rumors of her being difficult to work with), as is the unvarying quality of her performance.

Virtually a contemporary of Streisand, Diana Ross, born in 1944, took a different road to stardom as a member of the Supremes, one of the groups that was a major part of the Motown label's "Sound of Young America" in the 1960s. Where Barbra's sound was safe, continuing a tradition of show tunes and cabaret that dated back a few decades, Motown was eager to offer something new that spoke directly to the kids—that was the label's trademark. The Supremes were their biggest female stars, and as the leader, Diana was the most prominent, the one the cameras and interviewers always focused on. It wasn't too long before they were known as Diana Ross and the Supremes, then, six years after their first number 1 hit, Diana Ross took what seemed to be the next logical step, and went solo.

With her familiar name and the powerful backing of Motown, she was an immediate success, scoring hits, playing a series of shows at Caesar's Palace in Las Vegas, and making movies—*Lady Sings the Blues* (in which she portrayed jazz singer Billie Holiday) and *Mahogany*—all of which contributed to make her "the black Streisand," albeit with a slightly hipper image. With a tremulous, vulnerable voice, she had always been a natural for ballads such as "Touch Me in the Morning," although she, too, found some hits with upbeat, credible dance music, most notably "Muscles" and "Upside Down." For the last few years, Diana has been absent from the charts and the screen, not through any lack of success, but because of extended time away to raise the family she's had with her Norwegian businessman husband, Arne Naess.

When Barbra Streisand duetted on "No More Tears (Enough Is Enough)" with Donna Summer, it was a true sign of acceptance for the "Disco Diva," Donna Summer, who came to prominence in the mid-seventies with "I Feel Love," a song that was essentially a prolonged series of orgasmic noises over an electronic beat, and which heralded the first blast of the disco assault on the American mainstream. Although LaDonna Andrea Gaines was born only six years after Streisand, her material made her seem far younger than her new partner, and younger even than Diana Ross. Raised in Boston, Massachusetts, she grew up singing, idolizing Mahalia Jackson, and singing with gospel groups—a style that would be evident in some of her later work.

Donna auditioned for a role in *Hair* on Broadway, but was instead offered a chance to join the play's road company, which took her to Germany, where she met and married Helmut Sommer. After their divorce she anglicized his name and remained in Munich with her daughter Mimi, performing with the Vienna Folk Opera and singing backup at Giorgio Moroder's MusicLand Studios. If any one person can be deemed responsible for the disco phenomenon, it was Moroder, and once he began working with Summer as a lead singer, he created something that, for a few years at least, changed the face of popular music across the world.

"Love to Love You Baby"'s success labeled Summer as "the First Lady of Lust" and "Disco's Aphrodite," an image she hated, and actively worked to change. Moving back to the States, she had a number 1 hit with Jimmy Webb's lush ballad, "MacArthur Park," before returning to up-tempo songs like "Hot Stuff" and "Bad Girls," both of which also managed to climb to the top spot. The eighties began well for Donna, bringing more hits—including the duet with Streisand—but as disco's popularity faded, so did hers, and she disappeared from the record scene.

The woman to follow her came along in 1984, someone who aimed to eclipse everyone who'd gone before her—Madonna. Born in 1958 in Detroit, Michigan, Madonna Louise Veronica Ciccone was more a trained dancer than a singer; in fact, she won a dance scholarship with the Alvin Ailey troupe in New York before changing her mind and running off to Paris, where she managed to find work as a backup singer. Once back in the States, the Material Girl began working on her own music, and soon had a contract with Seymour Stein's Sire label.

From her very first record Madonna was the new Queen of Dance Music (as disco was called in the eighties), becoming known as much, if not more, for her outrageousness as for her music. Her costumes (underwear as outerwear, for example, or the wearing of large crucifixes) influenced girls across the country and across the world. She was perhaps the first artist, male or female, to fully realize the possibilities of the video format and the fledgling MTV network, and she utilized them to the point where she is probably more associated with them than any other performer. Her records sold—and continue to sell—in the millions, as she built a very public personality.

Each new action seemed specifically designed to stir up controversy (the video for "Like a Prayer," with its religious symbolism and tale of interracial love, or "Justify My Love," with its gender-bending action), and helped increase her record sales, even as her risqué concert performances brought more publicity and threatened jail for their star (although, noticeably, she has never been convicted of anything).

Madonna's impact on the music industry has been undeniable and enormous. She was selling more albums and singles than any other artist at the time. She had her finger on the popular pulse, and she knew how to manipulate the media, which she did in a masterful manner. It was an unstoppable combination, and it's one she continues to work with a very careful, calculating, and extremely successful eye.

THE COMMON FACTOR among these artists is the powerful presence, or personality, they can put across—not just in concert, or on television or in a video—but on disc. Each one can, to use an old phrase, "sell" a song with her voice, and make it real. It's a rare quality, and when a performer has it, audiences respond in droves.

By the time Mariah left home, the latest pop diva had become firmly entrenched at the top of the charts: Whitney Houston. Born August 9, 1963, she'd been performing regularly in clubs since her mid-teens, and at the age of twenty she was signed to a worldwide contract by music mogul Clive Davis of Arista Records, who spent two years grooming her and selecting material for her debut. Whitney had music in her genes—her mother is Cissy Houston, a soul and gospel singer, and her cousin is Dionne Warwick; she called Aretha Franklin "aunt." Like Donna Summer, Whitney had grown up singing in gospel choirs, and by the time she was twelve she was recording as a backup singer for name artists like Chaka Khan and Lou Rawls.

Her first album took off slowly—even the label expected it

to sell no more than 150,000 copies—but two number 1 singles ("Saving All My Love for You" and "How Will I Know") propelled it to the top of the *Billboard* charts, and to platinum status. A year later, her second album debuted at number 1—the first time a female artist had managed such a feat—and stayed there for eleven weeks. At that point Whitney had not only arrived, she was virtually dominant on the scene. Her voice had power, a wide range, and she was equally comfortable with emotional ballads and dance songs—in other words, she fulfilled all the requirements of a pop diva.

From there her success only grew, managing more than ten number 1 U.S. singles, as well as a number of hit singles in Britain. Her movie debut in *The Bodyguard,* with Kevin Costner, made that film into a smash, with its soundtrack album, featuring "I Will Always Love You," becoming a worldwide multi-platinum seller, moving 35 million copies across the globe. It's interesting to note that a music publisher once offered to send one of Mariah and Ben's songs to Whitney. Mariah refused; no one else was going to sing *her* hits.

Whitney was the performer that Tommy Mottola had to beat. Columbia had Barbra Streisand, still the undisputed Queen of Pop Divas, but she rarely released albums anymore. It was obviously a market with huge potential, and Mottola wanted Columbia to have a share of it—more than that, they *needed* a share of it. He had to find a new star, what the industry terms a "baby act," with plenty of talent and potential, that he could work with and push in just the right way.

ON A CHILLY Friday night in November 1988, Brenda was trying to persuade Mariah to go with her to a music-business party. Mariah wasn't crazy about socializing—her hectic work and recording schedules left her tired, and besides, clubs and parties always tended to be smoky, which aggravated her throat. But Brenda insisted. It was Friday night, they needed a break. There'd be food there. And finally Mariah gave in.

Several executives from CBS Columbia, Brenda's parent label, were there, including Tommy Mottola and Jerry Greenberg. Toward the end of the evening Mariah managed to pluck up her courage and approached Greenberg with her tape. But, even as she reached out to give it to him, another hand came down and snatched it away—Mottola's. A few minutes later, he left the party, and so did Mariah and Brenda. It was, Mariah decided, another waste of time. She'd probably never hear anything. But at least someone at the top of the organization would listen to her—if he ever bothered to play it.

From here the story has more or less passed into the folklore of the music business. On his way home in the limousine, Mottola took the tape from his pocket and slipped it into the cassette deck. After hearing just two of the tape's four songs, he instructed his driver to turn around and return to the party. He looked around for the singer, but didn't see her. As if she were Cinderella, she'd vanished.

The weekend followed, two frustrating days for Mottola, who was trying to track down the elusive vocalist. He knew she'd accompanied Brenda, but that was the only thing he knew about her. As Mariah told the story for *People*, "It [the tape] didn't have my name on it. He couldn't match up the voice with this Long Island kid in a football cheerleading jacket."

But as soon as Monday arrived, Mottola was on the phone, and the search for his Cinderella proved somewhat easier than Prince Charming's. Through Brenda K. Starr's management he was able to find Mariah's name and number, and without hesitation he called her.

"He left a message on my machine." Mariah continues the story. "I called back stuttering: 'Can I speak to M-mister M-mottola?' He said, 'I think we can make hit records.' I was like freaking *out*!"

That same afternoon, a very nervous Mariah, accompanied by her mother Patricia, sat in the office of the president of CBS Records, U.S.

Mottola said later, "When I heard and saw Mariah, there was absolutely no doubt she was in every way destined for stardom." He'd found his baby act, his new pop diva.

Ironically, at this time another record label began expressing some interest in Mariah, which led to a small bidding war for her talent. But Mottola knew her potential; he wasn't about to let anyone else stand in his way. CBS had power, and he wielded it.

Within a month, in December 1988, Mariah Carey signed a contract with CBS Columbia Records. Dreams do come true.

3

Whatever Mariah might have anticipated after she signed her contract, it probably wasn't what ended up happening to her during 1989. All of a sudden, instead of waitressing, sweeping up hair, and quitting jobs to avoid being called "Echo," she was packing and repacking her suitcase as she alternated her time between long, intense hours in recording studios on the East and West coasts.

It was Don Ienner's idea. He was the new addition to the Columbia staff, lured over by Mottola from Arista, where he'd been a promotions man and witnessed the things that had made a star out of Whitney Houston. Which made him a natural to work with Mariah. "Tommy told me, 'She's incredible; you just won't believe how good she is.' As far as he was concerned, it was the Second Coming." And as soon as he heard her for himself, Ienner was quick to agree. He, too, saw the potential in that voice. It had the ability to cross over into every market; it was a gold mine. "For this particular time, she is my number one priority," he told *Rolling Stone,* adding with a remarkable degree of honesty, "We don't look at her as a dance-pop artist. We look at her as a franchise."

And that meant the label wasn't about to take any chances. Ienner selected a group of star producers, men with long, proven track records of hits. There was Ric Wake, an Anglo-American whose most recent success had been with dance artist Taylor Dayne, Rhett Lawrence, who had an extensive history of working with acts like Earth, Wind and Fire, Smokey Robinson, perhaps the king of the soul balladeers, and Epic's strongest act by far—Michael Jackson. And then there was

Narada Michael Walden, one of the hottest talents behind the mixing board. His credits filled pages, but lately included such superstars as Michael Bolton, George Michael (both CBS acts), and the woman perceived as Mariah's main competition, Whitney Houston.

None of this was in Mariah's career plan. What she wanted was for she and Ben Margulies to produce the record themselves. After all, they knew the material better than anyone. They knew the way they wanted the songs to sound. And, given a good studio and a good budget, rather than the cramped quarters and rudimentary equipment of Bedworks, they were sure they'd be able to achieve it. As Mariah put it, "I wasn't open to working with a superstar producer." It was a natural feeling. She and Ben had worked on this material for three years. They'd *created* it. The songs had come out of their ideas and improvisations. They'd taken the skeletons, the germs of tunes, and put flesh on the bones, working night after night, take after take, until they had what they considered a very good demo. And now, with the result of all those hours of labor so close to seeing fruition, the last stage was going to be taken away from them. As Ben resignedly told Fred Bronson, ". . . It's inevitably what happens, and you hope that people handle [the songs] with care."

Once the names had been selected, meetings had to be arranged, and the producers introduced to Mariah and her voice. Tommy Mottola contacted them all personally—a measure of the importance he placed on this project. Narada Michael Walden promised to sit down with her when he was in New York. When that time came, he found her to be "very shy" and a fan of George Michael (a sound choice, given that Walden had been his producer). Still, it offered a starting point for their working relationship.

When Rhett Lawrence received the call inviting him to New York, all he was told was that the singer was eighteen and possessed "the most incredible voice you've ever heard."

On arriving and hearing her tape, he was forced to agree. "I literally got goose bumps on my arms when I heard her sing. I couldn't believe the power and maturity in her voice."

Ric Wake had a similar assessment when Mottola played him Mariah's demo tape. "It was obvious that she was great— she was amazing." Their meeting occurred on a Wednesday; Mottola asked if he could begin working with her the next day. As it happened, he could. Mariah appeared at his house, and things clicked between them—their very first writing session produced "There's Got to Be a Way," which would end up on the album.

For all that Mariah had aspired to produce herself, she happily and gratefully accepted the label's choices. As she later put it, "They did put me with different producers that they wanted to have me work with, and this being the first album, I took a certain amount of direction from the record company. You know, they are taking a chance." At the same time, she stated her goals for the future in no uncertain terms: "Ideally, though, I'd like to be involved with everything." Ric Wake, at least, was given a cassette containing demos of twelve songs that Mariah and Ben had penned together. For such a young, new pair it was an impressive collection, and several of the tunes would end up, rerecorded, on the album. Musically they were elaborate constructions and, as Ben said, "They were very close to what's on the album, if not almost exactly"—a tribute both to his ability and the amount of effort expended by the pair. Lyrically, Mariah tended to dwell on relationships. At least, that was her metaphor. The songs weren't "necessarily" about them; she was merely putting the events of her own life into a context that everyone could relate to.

Signing that contract proved to be an inspiration for Mariah and Ben. Within a week of putting her name on the dotted line, the ink barely dry, the two had written something new. Again, it seemed to be concerned with romance, but actually it was a celebration of their very recent good fortune, a song called "Vision of Love." It found its way onto the CBS tape that circulated to the producers.

However, there was still more writing to be done, and for this the company paired Mariah with her producers. She approached it all gamely. With Walden and Wake she worked in New York (although the recordings with Walden were done at Tarpan Studios in San Rafael, California). For Lawrence, she traveled to Los Angeles. It was there that he heard the demo for "Vision of Love," and realized its potential as a hit, but not as it currently stood: ". . . a fifties sort of shuffle." Mariah needed a more contemporary sound than that. So Lawrence, Mariah, Ben, and Chris Toland worked together on the arrangement in the studio. The tempo was changed, session musicians brought in to add guitars and bass (although Ben received credit for drums and programming on the final track), and Mariah recorded a new lead vocal. Her original vocal from the demo wasn't scrapped, though; it remained in the song as the second vocal in the chorus. Then, with some additional studio gloss from Narada Michael Walden, it was finished.

"There's Got to Be a Way" was the product of that first writing session between Mariah and Ric Wake. ". . . [I]t went from there," he remembered later in an interview. "We did four songs together." This was the only fruit of those joint compositions to make it onto the record, however, produced by Wake and Walden.

"I Don't Wanna Cry" came about in the writing time Mariah and Narada Michael Walden spent together. They'd worked on several songs, then he decided to "slow the tempo down" and try to create one of "those 'crying' type of ballads" that descended in a direct line from gospel music, and which he'd heard so often while growing up. Once it was on tape, he had a firsthand chance to see the standards of perfection that Mariah imposed on herself. Walden was perfectly happy with what they had; it was all in the can, and he believed Mariah was pleased with it, too. Then she called him. There was one line that, on repeated plays, troubled her. She'd had a better idea, and she wanted to change it. Which she did, not once, but two or three times as Walden flew the tapes to her in New York. Not only did she fix the line, she had some more ideas, and added them. Finally Walden had to call her and say, "Look, I used your lick on that thing because you like it, but the other stuff you're adding on, you really don't need." It took him a little while to convince her. But, as an experienced producer, he remained gratified by her professional attitude. ". . . Mariah was nineteen, twenty years old, making her first album. She really wanted it to be special."

(When asked to compare Mariah to his most recent superstar female act, Whitney, Walden was very diplomatic: "Both are tremendous singers," he said. ". . . I'm honored to be able to work with both of them.")

"Someday" was another Carey-Margulies composition—as was the majority of the completed album—and a tune that caught Ric Wake's attention from the first time he played the tape Tommy Mottola had given him. "I loved that song right from the beginning. . . . Then Mariah called me one day and said, 'I'd love to do it if you want to do it.' It was great—I'm glad she called me."

It had been one of the four songs on the demo tape Mottola plucked from Mariah's hand at the party, strong enough in its early form to impress the label president. Margulies described that version as "very simple and funky. It had a simplicity to it that kind of drew you into it," and he approved of the finished product (of which he was co-arranger), calling it "really simple and clean, and the point came across."

Like so many of the pieces they wrote, it began as an improvisation—in this case over a bass-and-drum line—a dance groove in the New Jack Swing/hip-hop vein. While Ben tried out chord changes on the keyboards, Mariah would find vocal melody lines and choruses. Then, as Ben recorded the instrumental track, working with synthesizers, sequencers, drum machines, and computers, she'd be busy completing a set of lyrics.

But even with all the planning and expensive technology, happy accidents could—and did—happen in the studio. Mariah recounted one of these, while she was working with Ric Wake and Ben on the vocal for "All In Your Mind": "I was using my upper register. . . . What happened was at the end of it, I did these vocal flips. When I was doing it, my voice split and went into a harmony. If you hear it, it splits. I was saying, 'Get rid of that,' but everyone said, 'No way, we're keeping that.' "

BEFORE THE RECORDING PROCESS was even complete, at Black Rock (the nickname for CBS Columbia's corporate headquarters in New York) meetings were being held and a plan formulated to ensure that the public would sit up and take a great deal of notice of Mariah Carey. The campaign to be mounted would be massive, the largest and most expensive the label had undertaken to "break" an artist since Bruce Springsteen was "marketed" to America in 1975 with his *Born To Run* album. And it was as closely organized as any military offensive.

Mariah had been given the designation of "priority artist"; in other words, making her a star was of paramount importance, and careers were on the line. As Jane Berk, former director of marketing for CBS Records, was quoted as saying in the *New York Times,* "We had numerous, numerous meetings about Mariah way in advance of the album's release. It was about carefully planting seeds in the industry and nurturing their development at every stage. It was very strategically planned. We went out on a limb, and it was worth taking the risk." Producer Ric Wake, who observed the furor, concurred: "There was so much momentum, and everyone was pushing so hard from every level. There were so many decisions being made."

Of course, it didn't hurt that Mariah had as her mentor the new head of the label's domestic operations. When the boss speaks, everyone underneath is very likely to listen, then jump as high as possible.

The marketing plan for Mariah was decidedly unusual. The way to do things, it was decided, was to put her before people with a great deal of influence, at the convention of the National Association of Recording Merchandisers (NARM) in Los Angeles in the spring of 1990. This would introduce her to the buyers for all the nation's large record chains, a powerful group that controls the quantities ordered of each album, and which was therefore in a position to push a new artist. Her performance there was to be preceded by a specially-produced video presentation detailing her life and the making of her record. It was a bold move, but one that, if it was successful, would reap some very handsome dividends.

"The energy level in that room was astounding," Howard Appelbaum, vice president and head buyer of the Kemp Mill chain in Maryland, observed. But regarding Mariah's actual performance—where she was backed by the late Richard Tee on piano, and singers Patrique McMillan, Billy T. Scott, and Trey Lorenz—he was somewhat less enthusiastic, stating that she was "good, not incredible." But then, the pressure on Mariah was tremendous, and it was virtually her first public singing appearance. (Virtually, but not quite; a few weeks before, CBS had debuted her in an invitation-only soiree in New York—a boost for executives and senior sales representatives, the people who would be called upon to sell her talent. For that, Mariah was as close to solo as she would ever be, accompanied only by Tee.)

Following their game plan, Columbia capitalized on the exposure Mariah had gained at the NARM convention by sending her on a nine-city promotional mini-tour, which allowed both record-store and radio personnel to personally meet and hear her. The usual procedure for labels was to send out tapes and hope someone in a position of authority heard them. But in this case, no chances were being taken. As Jane Berk explained, "We wanted to make sure people listened to Mariah—so we sent her." A risky tactic, it seemed to work. After seeing her again, during her appearance in Philadelphia, Appelbaum increased his chain's order for her album. And, following her visit to San Francisco, that city's station began playing an advance copy of "Vision of Love" (claiming to be the first in the country to do so). This was an extremely encouraging sign, as the station was thought of as a leader in the industry, which meant that others would soon be playing the song.

On the road, Mariah was accompanied by Patrique, Billy, and Trey, a group who not only kept the atmosphere lighthearted, but helped make this new, tense experience bearable for Mariah. What was essentially a boring venture—touring—became fun for her as they cracked jokes, argued, and gossiped around her.

She'd met them during the sessions for the album, when she recorded "There's Got to Be a Way" during February, which employed Billy T. Scott and his ensemble as part of the group of backing vocalists. (Billy also appeared on "All In Your Mind.") Trey was a friend of one of the vocalists and came to the studio. As Mariah recalled, "I heard someone singing all the high, top notes with me, and I'm like, 'Who is *that*?' I turned around and it was Trey." It was the beginning of a beautiful friendship.

NOW, WITH THE RECORD COMPLETE, all ten tracks of it, and the promotional tour under way, Mariah should have been focusing on the present. But that wasn't her style. Although her first disc hadn't even reached the stores yet—the mastering was finished, and it was being pressed—she was looking ahead to her next album. She and Ben had even written the first song for it, when she was back in New York for the weekend.

Traveling again, and surrounded by the upper echelon of label executives—Tommy Mottola, Don Ienner, Bobby Colomby—she played them the rough work tape she and Ben had put together of "Love Takes Time." It was plain, even crude, just piano and voice, but its impact was undeniable. The consensus was universal: "This is a number one record. You have to put this in that album." It wasn't exactly what Mariah wanted to hear. After too many grueling months in the studio, she was ready for a break.

But management was adamant. The song would be added to *Mariah Carey*, as the album had been titled. It was, quite literally, a case of stopping the presses. The demo was rushed to Walter Afanasieff, a studio whiz (he was responsible for the arrangements on the first three Whitney Houston albums— *Whitney Houston*, *Whitney*, and *I'm Your Baby Tonight*) whose work with Narada Michael Walden had so impressed Mottola and Ienner that they'd given him a job as an executive staff producer with Columbia. He was astonished at the opportunity. After all, she'd been working with top names, and he was still a relative unknown—at that point he'd never produced anything by himself. But time was of the essence, and he buckled down to the job. As it was, the rhythm and instrumental tracks were cut in one very long day. Then Walter stepped on a plane to New York and the Hit Factory studio where Mariah ". . . did her vocals. She did all the backgrounds, practically sang all night. . . . We came back to the studio that afternoon, and we had to fix one line that we needed to get from Mariah."

As soon as that was done, it was back to the West Coast, and Sausalito's The Plant studios, to mix the song into its final form. So, in a three-day marathon, from start to finish, "Love Takes Time" was done. Or that was what Walter thought. Columbia decided the vocals needed to be louder. He dashed back to the studio to remix the track. Time was quickly running out on his big break, and he knew it. But, as the clock ticked down to the deadline, he finished.

Even then, the first copies of *Mariah Carey* didn't list the track on the sleeve, although it was on the disc. "I don't know if they had to throw away a few hundred copies," Ben Margulies commented to Fred Bronson. But even if they had, Columbia thought it was worthwhile. They were certain the tune would be a smash.

OF COURSE, no album could be launched without a video, and with Mariah tagged as a "priority artist," that was particularly true. "This visual element was a very, very, very important part of exposing this artist," is the way Jane Berk put it, and while she was also referring to print ads, there's little doubt that she primarily meant video. For Mariah was prime material: young, attractive, photogenic, with a trailing mass of honey-blond curls, and statuesque (she stands 5′9″ tall). And networks like MTV and VH-1 had definitely been proved to have a huge impact on artists' careers—one only needed to look at Madonna to see that.

With "Vision of Love" selected as the first single, a video was ordered and shot. But the finished product failed to impress the Columbia top brass, and without any hesitation it was scrapped, and another ordered. "The special treatment really upset me," a disgruntled former label employee said. "They spend $200,000 on a video and Mariah doesn't like it. No big deal." One source estimated the total cost of both videos at $450,000, a figure refuted by Ienner ("Total bullshit")—although he did admit, "If we're gonna take the time and effort that we did with Mariah, on every level, then we're going to image her the right way. If it costs a few extra dollars to make a splash in terms of the right imaging, you go ahead and do it."

Luckily, the new clip, produced by Ron Kay, satisfied everyone. The last piece was in place.

JUNE 1990 was a very busy month for Mariah Carey, as the marketing machine at Columbia moved into top gear. In record stores all across the country her face stared out from displays, singing into an old-fashioned square microphone. In *Billboard*, the music-industry trade paper, a total of five full-page ads were bought for her upcoming album. And, in a completely unprecedented coup, she was beamed into millions of homes, appearing before the first game of the 1990 NBA Finals to sing "America the Beautiful," a spot almost invariably reserved for established stars, and which indicated just how much muscle CBS was exerting—at Tommy Mottola's behest—on her behalf.

But the deluge of publicity didn't stop there; indeed, it was just beginning. As the "Vision of Love" video began airing in heavy rotation on MTV, Mariah was on national television again—not just once, but twice, guesting on both "The Arsenio Hall Show" and "The Tonight Show." All the stops were pulled out for this one. As a rather bewildered Mariah said, almost apologetically, "I didn't get the chance to work my way up from clubs. And all of a sudden, I was on 'Arsenio Hall.' It's scary."

She didn't really need to worry. Columbia had done everything in its considerable power to assure her success, and on June 2, when "Vision of Love" entered the *Billboard* Hot 100 at number 73, followed on June 30 by *Mariah Carey* debuting on the Album 200 at number 80, it seemed they'd done their job quite effectively. Exactly *how* effectively was only discovered a few weeks later as both records continued to climb the charts.

On August 4, 1990, "Vision of Love" reached its peak at number 1 on the *Billboard* Hot 100, where it lasted for four weeks. Then its parent record hit the top of the album charts, beginning a remarkable run of twenty-two consecutive weeks in that position. (In the U.K. it would debut at its highest position, number 6.) Mariah dedicated the record to her sister Alison (by this time a housewife, still living on Long Island), but took great care in the acknowledgments to thank everybody who'd helped her along the way—from Patricia to the Columbia staff—not forgetting the creator of her gift, God. Never selfish with her gratitude, she didn't want anyone to be missed.

Mariah Carey had made her splash. And it was a very, very big one.

AS MARIAH HAS POINTED OUT, "I make pop music," and that's exactly what *Mariah Carey* was. From ballads to dance beats, it traversed the spectrum of popular music, and infused it all with an overtone of the gospel sounds she loved.

"Vision of Love," the leadoff track, was the perfect introduction to her voice. An ideal slow-dancing tempo, it still managed to swing, with Mariah's backing vocals (herself multitracked) answering her lead, which, on the final chorus, flew toward those trademark high notes before the instruments dropped out, leaving her to sing her way to the tune's climax alone.

"There's Got to Be a Way" was, lyrically, a piece of social concern about some of the ills in our society—homelessness, apartheid, bigotry (a subject close to Mariah's heart from her childhood), and famine. Restrained in the verses, the chorus had a "churchy" feel, mostly due to the backing vocals, which began to take off before the middle instrumental break, then soared at the key change close to the song's end as Mariah began to demonstrate fully the extent of her range, flitting through the upper register like a bird.

The ballad "I Don't Wanna Cry"—reminiscent in both rhythm and arrangement of Wham!'s "Careless Whispers"—opened with an attractive acoustic guitar line, then featured the powerful lower end of Mariah's range, one which had exactly the right dramatic power for such an emotional song, with its clever pause beat as emphasis before the last chorus. Equally soothing and draining, it served notice of the timeless quality in Mariah's voice.

"Someday," four tracks into the disc, was the first dance song; given the reputation that Mariah had (wrongly) acquired as a dance artist (or "dance 'droid" as one critic disparagingly put it), that might have been a surprise. But her performance was more than credible, even if this didn't offer her the challenge of the slower material. Over a bouncy, highly percussive beat, the melody bubbled, going into a soft, double-tracked rap before fading out over a chorus and Mariah's piercing high note.

"Vanishing" stood in complete contrast, utterly stark, just piano and Mariah's voice. She was able to produce the track herself—as she'd hoped to do for the whole album—and its intimacy stood in counterpoint to what she saw as "too much production" on the rest of the record. The gospel influence was particularly strongly evident here, with the rougher feel of the keyboard and a multitracked choir of Mariahs offering background vocals. While many critics just ignored the tune in their reviews, Alan Jackson of the prestigious *London Observer* deemed it *the* "outstanding track"; and, indeed, its very sparseness adds considerably to its simple power.

"All in Your Mind" was another ballad, one based around a strong, memorable chorus, which briefly showcased the extreme high end of Mariah's vocal reach. (Probably not since the late Minnie Riperton had anyone managed to reach so high a note on record.) Built around some basic keyboard arpeggios—played here by Ben Margulies—the two short verses merely acted as bridges between choruses, the song's real muscle.

It led into "Alone In Love," a Rhett Lawrence–produced ballad. Other than the synthesized instrumentation, this seemed, like the previous track, almost out of place on a nineties record, having far more the feel of a timeless standard. That could actually be said for much of *Mariah Carey*; the basis of its music was not in contemporary fads and fashions, but rather the material looked backward for its inspiration, to soul, some jazz, and especially gospel. In that regard, its success definitely bucked the trends, and sent a hopeful sign for the future.

A guest slot by Living Colour's guitarist Vernon Reid, blasting an Eddie Van Halen–style solo, opened "You Need Me," a dance track that gained its impact through a poppish chorus, studio effects on the vocals, and a powerful, concise middle guitar break.

"Sent from up Above" slowed the tempo slightly, with an arrangement that owed a great deal to seventies soul, particularly softer bands like the Chi-Lites, but with some nineties technological touches to brighten its appeal.

The penultimate track, "Prisoner," was utterly contemporary, the most upbeat piece on the album. Opening with a low rap, it kept a vibrant dance bpm (beats per minute) throughout, more or less pulling the words and melody along to the rhythm.

And then, finally, there was the song that stopped the presses: "Love Takes Time," another Carey-Margulies ballad, with a chorus that slipped into the brain and wouldn't go away. It fitted very well into the overall context of *Mariah Carey,* both musically and thematically, and certainly presented a stronger finish to the disc than "Prisoner" would have done.

Whether the album would have ended up doing as well without the label's gigantic marketing push is one of those questions that can never be answered. It utilized the best talents available, both in producers and session musicians, and the arrangements achieved exactly what was intended—they served as a backdrop for Mariah's voice, which was (as it should be) the record's focal point. While all the songs were strong, it was the ballads that better suited Mariah and brought out her personality, something Columbia obviously realized, as the slower songs comprised the majority of the disc. The

dance music, as so often happens in that genre, tended to sub-
merge her in the beat.

But perhaps the greatest strength of *Mariah Carey* was that
it didn't target any one specific audience. There was enough
variety on it to appeal to almost everyone. That it did just that
was evident when the single "Vision of Love," and the album,
topped not only the pop charts, but also the R&B and Adult
Contemporary charts, fully vindicating Tommy Mottola's
judgment in signing her to the label, and causing him to say,
"Mariah is one of the greatest singers ever."

The reviewers were quick to pick up on Mariah's astonishing range as the album's selling point—"all seven octaves of
it," as David Gates wrote in *Newsweek,* "from purring alto to
stratospheric shriek. Up in this dog-whistle register, she can
shape a scream into precise, synthesizer-like phrases." He did
note, however, "She has the good taste not to overuse this de-
vice, but how could anyone—especially a twenty-year-old—
resist showing off just a little?"

New York Newsday took a similar tack: "Young pop singers
with such extensive ranges often sacrifice emotion for technique, and there are times on Carey's debut album . . . when
that's the case. She'll accelerate into upper-register notes that
sound like high-pitched whistles. . . . But for the most part
Carey keeps her technique in check and uses her voice in service of the song." Hillel Italie waxed rhapsodic about Mariah's
vocal agility: "This is a voice that can probably shatter glass
and put it back together, that sounds as if she's taking the
words and twirling them over her head like a cowboy with a
lasso." And an enthusiastic review in *People* cited her "extraor-
dinary control, driving power, lovely pitch, and wide range,"
and added that she "has one of those voices that could probably be entertaining singing the phone book."

However, the praise wasn't completely unreserved. *Newsweek*'s Gates wasn't impressed by the songs, which, he
thought, "range from banal love complaints to a banal save-
the-world anthem." This was echoed by *People,* where Ralph

Novak believed "she would have profited from outside help," and that the album, "striking as it is, could have been spectacular with better raw material."

From the sales figures, though, the public obviously had no complaints about the raw material. *Mariah Carey* quickly went platinum (1 million copies sold), and would eventually go on to sell more than 6 million copies. In fact, this debut by Columbia's pop diva outsold *I'm Your Baby Tonight* by Arista's darling, Whitney Houston, by more than 2 million copies, a clear indication that Mariah was stealing some of her fans away.

It wasn't only the album that continued to sell. When "Vision of Love" vanished from the charts, "Love Takes Time" was there to take its place (coincidentally, both entered the Hot 100 at number 73), spending two weeks at number 1. Following that, it was the turn of "Someday," which lasted at the top spot for another two weeks, beginning on March 9, 1991; then "I Don't Wanna Cry," which was there for yet another two weeks. That run of hit singles was just as remarkable as the album sales; it made Mariah the first act since the Jackson Five to have her first four singles top the charts, something notably not achieved by Whitney, or by any of the other pop divas who had preceded her.

THE IDEA OF PERFORMING scared Mariah. She'd made no secret of the fact that she was essentially introverted. "I'm not into performing," she told Stephen Holden in the *New York Times.* "I have to make myself do it because it comes with the territory." But as the album and single rose through the charts, there was one live commitment, made earlier, that she had to fulfill. The Camel Summer Jam, held at Shoreline Amphitheater in Mountain View, California, was probably the single largest R&B/soul event of the year.

More than ten acts comprised the bill on August 5, 1990, the day after "Vision of Love" hit number 1. They included Tony! Toni! Toné!, Johnny Gill, Bell Biv Devoe (who were all certainly quite famous in their own right)—and the headliner was MC Hammer, whose "U Can't Touch This" had been a monster hit (although he would quickly disappear from sight, attempting to return in 1994 in full fake gangsta fashion). For Mariah, whose experience of live work had been limited to small showcases or television, it must have been daunting to suddenly find herself standing in front of thousands of people, having to perform—and as a support act, at that! By all accounts she acquitted herself well, overcoming whatever nervousness she felt to deliver a short but powerful set which, naturally, included a well-received rendition of the nation's biggest song. But, notably, she wouldn't follow up this show with more live work in front of an audience (except for taping MTV's "Unplugged" program and "Showtime at The Apollo") for more than three years.

WITH THIS GIGANTIC SUCCESS came the photographers and reporters. Everyone suddenly wanted to write a feature or take a picture or have a piece of her. She was hot. But unlike so many who view success as a license to go wild, Mariah continued her quiet, low-key approach to life. No social whirl, no nightclubbing, no evenings of photo opportunities for the paparazzi. Her biggest indulgence was a new car—a Mustang convertible—and a new place to live, where she didn't have to sleep on the floor or share with roommates.

She didn't even really move that far—just to New York's Upper East Side, where she found a one-bedroom apartment with a stunning view on the twenty-first floor of a high-rise building—a place to live with her two Persian cats, Ninja (all black) and Thompkins (all white), and which she could decorate with her Marilyn Monroe posters. Monroe, another star who'd experienced a poor childhood, and whose film career as the nation's sex symbol ended tragically in the early sixties with her suicide, was long a fascination of Mariah's. A friend disclosed, "Aside from the negative aspects of her life, she sort of idolized her. She liked the overall concept of being famous and the way Marilyn Monroe came to fame."

And Mariah was certainly famous enough herself these days; the star she'd prophesied to her teachers and school counselor that she'd be. As her best friend Patricia Johnson said, ". . . [S]he always did what she said she was going to do."

Not that fame offered her any greater opportunity to relax. "Vision of Love" had a video, and each new single demanded another, which represented hours of work and even more hours of boredom. For "Love Takes Time" she spent "most of the time preparing for the video in the trailer," as rain kept interrupting the shoot.

The final, acceptable clip for "Vision of Love" kept Mariah on a fairly stark stage set, before a backdrop of speeding clouds, an eerily-lit sky, and a single tree with a swing. The overall simplicity of the design focused attention where it belonged—on her and on the song. It *worked.* In all likelihood we will never know what the scrapped version looked like, but this made it all irrelevant. In terms of presenting a new artist, it was perfect, unpretentious, evocative of solitude, loneliness, and, somehow, of hope.

"Love Takes Time" was even more romantic, shot in soft-focus black and white on a beach. Translating the song to a video concept was an arduous task, but Walter Maser did a splendid job. The empty phone booth, with its receiver dangling and twirling, stood as a particularly powerful image of lost love; and a heartbroken Mariah wandering along the sand, in and out of the surf, only accentuated that idea.

"I Don't Wanna Cry" again found Mariah as the sole face on the screen, bathed in red and orange lights as she walked around a stage. Behind her, instruments and microphones were set up, as if for a performance, once more highlighting the loneliness of the ballad's lyrics.

As befits its outgoing, upbeat tempo, "Someday" featured a more substantial cast. Mariah herself took a hand in the planning of this video, which was shot at a high school in Bayonne,

New Jersey. She'd come up with the original concept, of a young girl (based on herself) and a young boy, then collaborated with director Larry Jordan, adding more ideas until they had a completed storyboard. Working and being able to interact with others on the set, particularly a group of six- to twelve-year-olds, was "the most fun" she'd experienced in making a video. It was also gratifying for her to be able to include Larry Wright, a "great" street drummer who had come to her attention via a PBS documentary. Prominently featured among the kids was a hyperactive six-year-old hip-hop dancer who stole the spotlight whenever he was on camera.

The collected video soon found commercial release as *Mariah Carey—The First Vision*, and promptly entered both the U.S. and U.K. video charts. Featuring the clips for "Vision of Love," "Love Takes Time," "I Don't Wanna Cry," and an extended version of "Someday," it also contains an insightful interview with Mariah, offering some more details of her childhood and pre-stardom experiences, as well as footage shot during rehearsals for her "Saturday Night Live" spot on October 27, 1990 (where a happy Mariah clowns and warms up with Billy, Patrique, and Trey), and preparing for her performance on the "Showtime at The Apollo" television show. Playing at Harlem's famous Apollo Theater, which had at one time or another hosted all her soul-music idols, was a huge thrill for Mariah.

All of this helped to make the video special, but the highlight perhaps was the two songs filmed at an early showcase gig at New York's Club Tatou. Accompanied by a small group (piano, keyboards, bass drums, and Billy, Trey, and Patrique on backing vocals), Mariah sang "Vanishing" and "Don't Play That Song," a soul tune made famous "by the incomparable Aretha Franklin," whose influence on Mariah is obvious in the phrasing and dynamics of the piece, and the gospel manner in which she carries syllables across the line breaks and improvises upon the written melody lines.

* * *

ALL THE TRIUMPHS OF 1990 were marvelous, and at year's end came the crowning jewels, as Mariah found herself nominated for an astonishing *five* Grammys: Best Pop Vocal Performance, Female, for "Vision of Love"; Best New Artist; Album of the Year; Song of the Year (again for "Vision of Love"); and Best Album. This made her only the third person in the entire history of the Grammy Awards to be nominated for Best New Artist, Best Album, and Song of the Year in the same year. Not at all shabby for a rookie.

The 33rd Annual Grammy Awards was held at New York's Radio City Music Hall on February 20, 1990. The show was broadcast to sixty countries. Dressed in a short, tight black dress trimmed in silver, Mariah awaited the announcements of the winners in her categories, and also prepared for her own performance, as she appeared onstage to sing "Vision of Love" for an audience that would total many millions around the globe (this would later be available as part of the *Great Moments of the Grammys* collection).

As the evening wore on, and the count of winners and losers grew, Mariah made two more trips to the stage, where she collected Grammys for Best New Artist and Best Pop Vocal Performance, Female. The sheer delight on her face in the photographs taken afterward says it all. Not only had she been accepted by the public, she'd also been heartily embraced by the music establishment, joining a small, elite group of multiple-Grammy winners.

That alone could have been the icing on the cake. But within a month her new mantelpiece must have been crowded with trophies. The *Rolling Stone* Readers' Picks Music Awards named her Best New Female Singer. Then, on March 12, at the Fifth Annual "Soul Train" Awards, held at the Shrine Auditorium in Los Angeles, she walked away with three more awards—Best New R&B/Urban Contemporary Artist; Best

R&B/Urban Contemporary Single, Female; and Best R&B/ Urban Contemporary Album—as sure a sign as any that the African-American community had accepted her music. Then, just to round things off, Mariah and Ben took Song of the Year honors for "Love Takes Time" at the BMI 40th Annual Pop Awards dinner, held on May 19 at the Regent Beverly Wilshire Hotel in Los Angeles, with additional honors given for both "Vision of Love" and "Someday," while "I Don't Wanna Cry" received a citation. The additional effect of all these awards— most especially the Grammys—was to increase the reorders from stores for her album. With her name before the public again (as if it hadn't been there enough in the last few months!) there was an increased demand for her music.

HOWEVER, THE FULL MEASURE OF FAME is never complete until the backlash comes around. The press, it seems, delights in creating heroes and idols, only to promptly tear them down again as the full "truth" comes out.

In Mariah's case it began early, almost before she'd had the luxury of resting on the laurels of her success. The first thing was little more than rumor and innuendo—that she and Tommy Mottola were romantically involved. In mid-1990, it was true, Mottola and his wife of nineteen years, Lisa Clark Mottola, had signed a separation agreement, which allowed him generous visitation rights to their two children. But he was adamant in denying all the reports that linked him to Mariah in anything other than a business sense. Still, some said, there had to be an ulterior motive for all the attention he'd lavished on her career and the push Columbia had given her album . . . no smoke without fire.

As for Mariah, she really didn't want to talk about it. "There is not much that is sacred in this business," she said. "But to me, my private life is." When questioned, she did admit to having a boyfriend, but she was unwilling to offer any more details.

The other accusation leveled at her was far more serious. It was bandied around that Mariah was trying to exploit the black community by being yet another white singer attempting to sound black, a rip-off. *That* demanded immediate action, and interviews were quickly set up with two leading black publications, *Jet* and *Ebony*.

Such an attack must have been felt by Mariah on a very deep and personal level. After all, the scars of racial intolerance weren't that old. She'd seen it contribute to the breakup of her parents' marriage, and the misery it had caused both her brother and sister when they were growing up. And, while Mariah had never hidden her background, neither was it something she'd chosen to make an issue of. Why should it even be necessary? Couldn't people just accept her as she was—a person, Mariah Carey, the girl from Long Island? But, she explained, "Some people look at me and they see my light skin and my hair. I can't help the way I look, because it's me. I don't try to look a certain way or sing a certain way. I'm just trying to be me. And if people enjoy my music, then they shouldn't care what I am, so it shouldn't be an issue." And as she told *Ebony*, "If you look a certain way everybody goes, 'White girl,' and I'd go, 'No, that's not what I am.' "

The articles seemed to defuse the problem before it really took hold. But it must, at some level, have cast a minor pall on the year for her. All her life she'd had to cope with prejudice. Now, even with fame, she couldn't escape it entirely.

All in all, though, it really had been an amazing beginning. For her "the thrills [had] come in stages," which had moved very rapidly—seeing her album in the store, appearing on television, hearing her songs on the radio, being number 1 in *Billboard*! Why, exactly, had she struck such a deep, resonant chord with people? Yes, the marketing had helped tremendously, both in distributing her product and getting her name known, but the bottom line was, if people didn't like it, they wouldn't buy it, no matter how it was packaged. The annals of the music business are littered with names that were hyped for a while, only to fall by the wayside and become footnotes because, in the end, nobody bought their records.

Mariah was giving people what they wanted. She had a large amount of talent. That surely helped, but other talented performers had failed to connect. She'd been lucky, and that was virtually a necessity for success. She was young enough—when she collected those two Grammys she was still only twenty—for a large segment of the record-buying audience to easily relate to her. And she had dedication, an unwavering faith in her own ability. Yes, maybe she'd only really struggled for a year, but during that time she'd used almost every spare moment in service of her career.

In all probability the reason for her success was a combination of all those factors, mixed with her freshness. That she'd cowritten all her material was particularly important; after all, it's easier to invest your own words with emotion than someone else's, and people can tell, at some instinctive level, if that ache in your voice is real or faked. And it set her far apart from the other pop divas on the scene. She did not become just another singer who arrived at the studio, punched in her vocal, went home, then counted her royalty checks. She had a great deal invested in every note. With every song she was putting herself on the line, showing her heart, exposing her sadness or offering inspiration to others—a positive message, which, from a figure in the spotlight, can often do a vast amount of good.

What mattered, ultimately, was that she *had* succeeded. But while some people in the same position might have found their heads turned, Mariah was fine, her feet planted very firmly on the ground, thanks in large part to her mother, who'd filled her with very strong values, both social and artistic, and always bolstered her belief in herself. Mariah may have been proud of her album "for a first effort," but, like any true artist, she was "never satisfied with her work"; there was always something she could have improved or done differently. But, in the brief moment that she was able to rest her feet in one of many new pairs of shoes (or sneakers) and afford more than one outfit, the evidence of her perspective on 1990 was best summed up when she smiled and said, "It beats waitressing, right?"

It most certainly did. And this was only the beginning.

4

The question was, where did Mariah go from here? A number 1 album, four number 1 singles. How could she ever hope to top that? What should her next move be? Indeed, what was left to conquer? For most acts, the logical next step would be a massive tour, if not throughout the world, then at least a long string of dates in the U.S., in arenas and large halls, then maybe a few selected shows in England and Japan. It would consolidate the fan base that had been established and give the crowds a chance to see their idol in the flesh.

But Mariah, as she had said, was not inclined toward live performance. At least, not yet. She knew it was something she'd have to undertake eventually. Not yet, though. She liked the idea of traveling, but not the endless nights in hotel rooms. They affected her main asset, her voice, and that alone was a perfectly good reason to put it off. Without her voice she couldn't give a good show, and if she was going to do it, she was going to do it right. "I need a lot of sleep," she said, "and my songs are all strenuous." She had a very accurate gauge of her abilities, and, more importantly, her limitations.

Nor was she particularly comfortable with the amount of attention she'd been receiving since her rise to stardom. "I don't want to be about hype and media," Mariah explained, showing just how modest and self-effacing she was at heart. "I don't want to put myself in everyone's face and make them sick of me." That had happened before, to too many artists whose spell in the sun then proved all too brief. Mariah Carey was developing a *career* in music. She intended to be around for a long time, doing exactly what she loved—if not singing always, then songwriting. And, with seven million copies of her first album sold, there was no danger that she'd ever have to return to waitressing or sweeping up hair.

Mariah's solution to the dilemma of what her next move would be was to begin working on her next album. For her to even consider such a thing at this stage was highly unusual. Within the music industry, it was accepted wisdom to wait at least two years between records, letting each play out its sales potential before releasing a new one (which would pick up new fans, who'd then find their way to the earlier catalogue). This way, sales of each disc could be maximized without the market seeming to be saturated by an artist's product. In the sixties, things had been very different. Back then groups and singers usually put out two albums a year, generally "driven," or highlighted by, a couple of hit singles that would be included, with the rest of the material largely filler. The Beatles had altered that way of thinking. Writing their own songs (and being virtually the first to do so consistently) meant that every track on the album was strong, generating a demand for the long-player (LP) on its own merits. By the end of the decade, with the advent of AOR (album-oriented rock), the album slowly became far more important for sales than the single, eventually achieving dominance, and over the course of two decades the marketing process for it had become more and more sophisticated and refined. So what was Mariah's reason for being so different?

Columbia's decision to release a new Mariah Carey album "soon" was, they said, due to Mariah "growing so much from the last album." It was a perfectly believable situation in a singer and writer who was so young (just twenty-one!) and relatively new to the business. After all, Mariah must have learned a great deal during the year she'd spent in studios, recording *Mariah Carey,* and even more in the time since, spent promoting it.

* * *

THERE WAS, however, something which appeared to stand as a large stumbling block to all this—Mariah and Ben Margulies were no longer a writing partnership. A breach had occurred between them which would prove irreparable. The reason, reportedly, was that long before Mariah inked her deal with Columbia, she had signed a contract with Ben which entitled him to almost half of the money she earned from the album, as opposed to just half the royalties from the music-publishing rights of the songs they'd composed, to which he was, legally and morally, certainly entitled.

Looking back on the situation some time later, Mariah said sadly, "I blindly signed. Later, I tried to make it right so we could continue . . . but he wouldn't accept it." For his part, Ben placed the blame on the music business, and expressed the hope of "getting back together in the not-too-distant future. . . . Hopefully, art will prevail over business."

And that was the way five years of friendship, of struggle and tough times, and of eventual triumph over adversity, ended.

One must wonder, though, what part—if any—the label played in all this. Is it possible that they'd paid heed to the reviewers when they complained about the quality of the songs on *Mariah Carey*? Mariah and Ben had cowritten seven of those eleven songs. Granted, three of them had been smash hits, but Mariah was growing. Maybe it would be to her advantage to work with other people, to expand her horizons. She'd already proved she could do it—and very successfully.

COLUMBIA HAD ALREADY INDICATED that it was willing to give her some latitude, both in material and production. "She deserves it," Don Ienner said. "She has a great feeling of what's right and what's wrong." And Tommy Mottola had already predicted, "I'm sure she wants to do a lot more on her next album, make it more stark."

After a relatively short period of consideration, Mariah

began teaming up with a number of writers. There was the duo of David Cole and Robert Clivilles (of C + C Music Factory, whose "Gonna Make You Sweat" had been a huge hit, both on the charts and in the dance clubs), with an ability to write and produce strong up-tempo material, as evidenced by a number of gold records and positive reviews from respected critics. And, surprisingly, there was Walter Afanasieff, the man who'd produced "Love Takes Time" in such a rush. A Brazilian who'd immigrated to this country, he seemed an odd choice, having no track record of writing hit songs. But Mariah obviously felt relaxed and creative in his presence, and this was going to be her call—at least, within reason.

And then there was Carole King. She was a graduate of the Brill Building music factory of the early sixties, where, with partner Gerry Goffin, she'd churned out a series of pop hits like "Up On the Roof" and "Will You Still Love Me Tomorrow?" But then she'd walked away from that to become a remarkably popular singer/songwriter—her *Tapestry* album from 1971 sold over 13 million copies and stayed on the charts for an unbelievable 302 weeks.

Perhaps surprisingly, it was King who first approached Mariah, to ask if she'd be interested in recording a version of the Goffin-King song, "Natural Woman," which had been a big hit for Aretha Franklin. Mariah turned down the idea. Aretha, of course, was one of her idols, and since her recorded performance was already "untouchable," she felt there was nothing new she could bring to it. So, instead, Carole King left her home in Idaho to fly to New York for one day and have a writing session with this young singer.

What came out of it was a ballad entitled "If It's Over," which Mariah described as "a true collaboration." The two sat and traded musical ideas, and Mariah came up with a set of lyrics, with work continuing until they had what they both described as "a wonderful song." And King added, "I love her voice. She's very expressive. She gives a lot of meaning to what she sings." This was praise and acceptance, not just from a contemporary, but from a veteran who's heard literally thousands of other voices sing her songs.

That type of collaboration—sitting down, bouncing ideas off the other person—seems to be Mariah's favorite way of working. She'd done it with Ben for four years. It worked with Carole King, and it seemed to work once again with Walter Afanasieff. In him, Mariah appeared to find a substitute for Ben, someone who was eager to write with her, to the extent that he would use every spare scrap of time for the venture.

For them, the process had begun as early as late 1990, many months before any recording. Walter was involved in his latest project, producing Michael Bolton's newest album, spending long hours in the studio. But when breaks would occur—such as when Michael had to leave and play a few shows, or decided to take a short vacation—Walter took advantage of the opportunity to sit down and write with Mariah.

The creative sparks flew between them. He'd begin with an idea, something played on the keyboard, either a chord progression or a short instrumental line. In turn, this would inspire her with ideas for a vocal melody or some lines of lyrics. Then, as she would sing, Walter said, "I start playing to what she's singing." And things would continue until the piece was finished and Mariah was satisfied with the words she'd written.

It really was eerily similar to the way Mariah and Ben had worked. Perhaps the main difference was that Walter's keyboard ability and knowledge of music theory were much greater. He could translate Mariah's vocal sketches into reality at a much greater speed, with less guesswork.

It originally had been Tommy Mottola's idea to bring in David Cole and Robert Clivilles. It was a given that the new record would repeat the successful formula of mixing ballads and dance music, and who better for the dance music than the hottest team in the country?

As an established team, Clivilles and Cole already had their set way of working. They came to the writing session armed with plenty of ideas—"grooves" as they called them—and played them for Mariah, seeing which ones might work as the basis for songs. One decision they'd made right at the beginning was that they didn't want to emphasize Mariah's "high stuff." Although they knew it would be impossible to ignore it, they were both eager to steer clear of any criticism of trading on a gimmick. Instead, they planned to concentrate on bringing out Mariah's singing ability.

Mariah herself came to the second album with a few definite ideas. As Mottola had forecast, she wanted the sound to be more sparse, letting more space into the songs and allowing them to breathe. She was also quite determined to fight for her ideas, having given in to others' opinions too easily on *Mariah Carey*. ("I thought, 'Maybe they're right. They're big and famous and I'm just a new up-and-coming hopeful.' ") And she was also keen for the overall sound to have a greater Motown and gospel influence—the sounds her brother and sister had played when she was very young, and the music she'd gone on to discover herself. The gospel ideas had been there on the first album, but she wanted them deeper and stronger now.

More important than anything, though, was the fact that this time she'd have what she'd lacked before (but hoped for)—total involvement in the whole process, from writing to arranging to performing to producing. She'd be there every step of the way. And more than happy to take responsibility for her own music.

By the start of spring 1991, Mariah had a large collection of songs at the demo stage, which she and Walter then played for the executives at Columbia, so decisions could be made as to which ones should be given the real treatment. The new album, once again, would be slightly weighted toward ballads. It had worked last time, and the emphasis here was to be on refinement, not innovation. The ballads seemed to be Mariah's forte; they gave her a chance to *really* sing, be it in her lower register or unleashing those angelic high notes. They'd also generated the most interest in the press, which was a factor worthy of consideration. But any style Mariah attempted she seemed to master with both ease and grace. It increased her options for music.

So, armed with a list of tunes which the label had approved (there was never a shadow of a doubt about the inclusion of the Carey-King collaboration), Mariah once again found herself boarding planes and shuttling from coast to coast in pursuit of her art. Cole and Clivilles would produce the dance tracks with Mariah, and the other material would continue to be a joint effort between Mariah and Walter.

The good weather was just beginning as she went into the studio. Unfortunately, she wouldn't see too much of it, keeping her night-owl hours, working from early evening through until dawn, then sleeping the day away. It was, she said later, "like living in a cave." And recording studios can be that way—isolated, insulated rooms away from the real world, without windows, artificially lit. Each might have its own character, but there remains a sameness that covers them all: Skywalker Sound in Marin County, The Plant in Sausalito, or Skyline, Axis, Battery, or Right Track in New York.

Working on this album was certainly a full-time job for Mariah. Composing, singing, and producing weren't enough for her; she was also involved in arranging the tracks and singing most of the background vocals (something she'd done on the first album). But, as she'd admitted, she loved being in the studio, most particularly singing there, building up layers of her voice and playing them back, carrying on until she'd achieved exactly what she was searching for.

While she might have decided that "I still don't think of myself as a big deal," that wasn't the opinion of many others. Quite naturally, Columbia was eager for this disc to repeat the success of *Mariah Carey,* and her fans were anxious to hear more of her voice. Could she deliver the goods again? And could these new partnerships produce strong-enough songs?

* * *

THE ANSWERS TO THOSE QUESTIONS CAME—at least in part—when the first single from the new album was released and jumped into the *Billboard* Hot 100 on August 31, 1991, at number 35, the highest entry position of any of her singles to date. It was a bouncy dance tune—"Emotions," one of the four Carey-Cole-Clivilles collaborations—and also the album's title track. (Oddly, though, it wasn't originally planned as the first single; that was going to be "You're So Cold," the first song the trio completed together, which did end up on the record.)

The song's inspiration actually came from a group called the Emotions, who had scored their own number 1 hit in 1977 with "Best of My Love," a disco tune produced by Earth, Wind and Fire's Maurice White. Thoroughly likable, it didn't depend on any bass line or drum pattern, just a floating groove and a very memorable melody, and these were the qualities Mariah sought to emulate. "It definitely has the feeling from the Emotions," David Cole admitted, adding that it was Mariah who came up with the idea of using that band's name for the album title. ". . . [W]e all decided, 'No, why not?' . . . it's a great name for a song."

Six weeks later, on October 12, after the album had been released, "Emotions" was number 1, where it remained for three weeks. That gave Mariah a unique piece of chart history, being the first artist *ever* to have her first five singles all reach number 1, beating the Jackson Five's previous record of four, established twenty-one years before. It was a landmark achievement, and a very hopeful sign for the new album.

The single "Emotions" was followed by "Can't Let Go," which rapidly followed it onto the Hot 100. Sadly, it didn't quite manage to continue Mariah's amazing run of number 1 hits, peaking at a breath-catching number 2 as its predecessor, now a gold record, slipped down the Top Fifty.

"Make It Happen" was the third and final single from the album. With its catchy chorus, inspiring message, and bouncy beat, it seemed like a natural, rising up the chart through

March of 1992. However, it stalled at number 5, the lowest place to date for any of Mariah's singles. (Almost everything she's released has made at least the Top Five, a claim that virtually no artist of today—or any other era—can make.)

BY HER OWN STANDARDS, the album succeeded. *"Emotions* has a little bit of an older-type vibe, a Motown feel," she told *New York* magazine. It displayed the increased confidence that two years had brought to Mariah, both in her vocal style and her lyrics.

The critics approached it more cautiously than they had the first one, giving it more consideration, which, at the same time, meant viewing it more closely. She'd gone beyond the stage of being label hype to become an artist, and was about to be treated like one.

David Hiltbrand, writing in *People*, said, "The material here is stronger and the arrangements richer," even if "as on her debut, the song selection is somewhat uneven"—although he was willing to acknowledge "that Carey is truly a transcendent talent." Christian Wright, in *New York Newsday*, found that, at least on one cut, "she infuses a torchy and breathy croon with the sort of genuine passion that was completely missing from the first album," and noted that *"Emotions* uses simpler arrangements so that the voice is showcased as the most important instrument."

From those words it might be assumed that the reviewers thought that Mariah had more than adequately conquered the notorious sophomore jinx. However, they were still able to find plenty of faults. The most common one was that Mariah overused her now-famous upper register (which was odd, since she was actually quite sparing with it), and the other was that she approached "everything at maximum intensity, even ballads . . ."—or, as Arion Berger stated in *Entertainment Weekly*, she "reaches for epiphany on every cut," although he was good enough to concede that the album "ticks along like a

Swiss watch—finely tuned, glossily assembled, filled with precision instrumentals and spectacular vocal turns." He had nothing good to say about Mariah's lyrics, either, calling them "hackneyed high school poetry" which "for most of the album . . . either lament the recent departure of some cad or praise the next Mr. Right." For "The Wind," the album's last track, Christian Wright took a completely different view, feeling that "Carey has written moving lyrics."

All of that largely went to prove there were as many opinions as there were writers. The real judging would come from the record buyers, people who were willing to shell out hard-earned money for an album.

In all likelihood, no one probably expected *Emotions* to sell in the same vast quantities as *Mariah Carey,* let alone exceed it. Too little time had passed since her debut. She was, if anything, too much in the public eye. Mariah herself wasn't worried; she had her sense of security now. "If I wanted to stay home and write songs and make a moderate living, I could do that." It was the artistic satisfaction, not the commercial success, that was driving her.

In the final count, the sales performance of *Emotions* didn't even come close to *Mariah Carey,* ending up with a total of 3 million copies sold. While that might seem like a disappointment in comparison, it really wasn't. Out of the thousands of albums released each year—even by established, name artists—very, very few sell enough to dent the charts, even its lower rungs. To go gold (that is, to sell half a million copies) is a great achievement; to go beyond that, to platinum (one million copies sold) is rare; past that point, an album is far more than successful, it's a skyrocket.

It should also be remembered that the sales of *Mariah Carey* were helped by a very skillful marketing campaign, which was absent for *Emotions.* This record sold on Mariah's popularity, the success of its singles, and, most importantly, its own merit. Given those factors, it was an unqualified smash.

The record led off with the title track, already familiar from its position as a number 1 single. Over a frothy groove that owed far more to seventies disco than nineties dance music, Mariah gave a joyful lyric. She used that high end of her range, but its presence, while more reserved, was also stronger and a fully integrated part of the song's arrangement, where it had seemed more like an ornament before. This track was actually one of only two Carey-Cole-Clivilles compositions (the two other, faster tunes being credited to just Carey and Cole). As on all the other faster songs, David Cole played the keyboards, while Robert Clivilles contributed drums (as on *Mariah Carey*, most of the instruments on this release were synthesized), for a wonderfully bouncy feel.

"And You Don't Remember" allowed Mariah's gospel side to show. Gliding silkily over organ chord changes, and rising to a heartbroken, much rawer chorus, the sad melody reflected the words—a story of being duped and then forgotten by a boyfriend, one of those men who obviously promises the world then immediately goes on to the next girl. These two opening tracks showed that this album, for all its nineties instrumentation and technology, was going to achieve what Mariah had hoped, and have a sixties and seventies feel, not only the songs themselves, but the way they were performed. Except for three cuts where she'd collaborated with others, she was entirely responsible for all the vocal arrangements (she'd worked with her coproducers on the instrumental arrangements), and it was here, more than anywhere, that her influences showed—in the backgrounds, with their sweet, high harmonies that recalled black church choirs or the enthusiastic sounds of the young Motown bands.

"Can't Let Go" was pure, sad ballad, a pop song that could easily have been written in any decade from the fifties onward, but also had a hymnlike quality in its minor-chord changes, particularly in the introduction. Not that that was a bad thing; with only twelve notes in the musical scale, by now almost every tune has been written. And for this Mariah stayed with her huskier low range, letting the emotion in her voice convey the pain above a simple instrumental backing.

For "Make It Happen," Mariah wrote a set of very autobiographical lyrics, detailing the struggle and rough period she went through before being signed to Columbia (even down to the fact that she could only afford that single pair of holey sneakers!), and what kept her going through it all—her faith. That wasn't just a faith in herself and her talents, but also the ability to let herself go, to pray to God, and trust in what would happen. These were, by far, her most inspiring words to date, letting others know that whatever they were doing, no matter how difficult things were, with help they could win through. Musically it was a restrained dance beat, very Motownish, that owed more than a little to gospel, with a chorus—sung by Mariah, Trey, and Patrique—that rose gloriously from the verse to repeat and drive its very positive message home.

This was followed by what was probably the most anticipated song on the album, "If It's Over," the piece cowritten by Mariah and Carole King. It echoed the type of songs that had proved so powerful for Aretha Franklin in the late sixties— slow, but very soulful, and, again, full of that gospel sound that Mariah loved. Such material allowed Mariah to really tear loose and show what she could do—which in reality was far more than the vocal gymnastics which seemed to comprise her reputation so far. From a deep rumble to a high wail she covered five octaves wonderfully as the power of the tune built. The backing vocals—which once more had those church harmonies—filled out the sparse melody, as did the stately horns, which entered toward the end. Indeed, the whole song was essentially a showcase for Mariah, and so beautifully out of time on a modern album that it came across as something quite new. It also showed that further collaborations between Mariah and Carole would be quite in order, and more than welcome. Maybe someday it'll happen. . . .

"You're So Cold" seemed to come across as four parts Emotions (the group), and one part Paula Abdul, the dancer-turned-singer who had some success before abruptly vanishing from the music scene. From a grandiose piano-and-vocal introduction it sailed into the chorus, driven throughout by David Cole's pianowork, the bubbly, snaking rhythm belying the angry lyrics, and the upbeat tone of voice. Once more, this didn't seem like a nineties song, but something that wouldn't have been out of place in the early disco era, and certainly a pleasant relief from the bass-heavy hip-hop thumpings that were filling the radio. The first song that Mariah and David Cole penned together, it had been considered as the album's lead single, but was eventually dropped in favor of "Emotions," and remained just an album track.

"So Blessed" was a sweet, touching song that displayed Mariah's softer side. Its tune recalled both fifties pop ballads and the soul changes of songs like "When a Man Loves a Woman," as it sailed over layers of Hammond organ and synthesized strings. The joyful, glad words found their expression in Mariah's smooth, restrained singing, which sounded as if she was performing with a happy smile on her face.

"To Be Around You" was far more staccato. In his *Rolling Stone* review, Rob Tannenbaum accused David Cole of using "pumping house keyboards," but none of that had really seemed to be in evidence on *Emotions'* faster tracks, and certainly not here. He did, however, also remark that some of the material appeared to "recycle the chords of Cheryl Lynn's 'Got to Be Real.' " While this song pays tribute to that in its overall feel and arrangement, there is no real recycling or rewriting involved. With the spoken voices at the end, this track has an uplifting party sense, a sense of well-being that the words (about an attentive lover) conjure up.

The quiet changes of "Till the End of Time," with its gentle, almost lullaby melody, would give the impression that it was the final track, the winding-down of a night. It was a love song, directed at a boyfriend, but with the overall impression that Mariah was actually saying it to herself, rather than to him in the flesh. As it was, it worked perfectly as a segue between the rest of the album and its real last cut, "The Wind."

"The Wind" was originally a jazz instrumental, written by Russell Freeman in the 1950s, which Walter Afanasieff had discovered on a record by the pianist Keith Jarrett. When Walter played it for Mariah, the melody touched her, inspiring a gorgeous set of lyrics about a friend who had died in a drunk-driving accident.

Musically it was the greatest challenge she'd yet undertaken. She'd mastered gospel, but jazz, with its slippery chords and tumbling changes, was altogether a different matter. It required a subtle touch, and, to put the emotions of this particular set of words across, a great deal of delicacy. Mariah handled it superbly, holding back, and moving to the swing of the beat, letting it direct her and not trying to push it. The piece also gave Walter a rare chance to shine, embellishing the vocal with runs on piano and synthesized vibes. The whispery voice mingled with the instruments to create a melancholy mood that became the perfect closer, something to surprise listeners (as "Vanishing" had done on her debut), and to impress, making it clear that, with time, Mariah could have a strong future as a jazz singer.

More than anything, what *Emotions* showed was Mariah's remarkable consistency. *Mariah Carey* hadn't been a fluke; she was a reliable, professional performer, one who could deliver the goods in any style. It also demonstrated not just that she'd grown, but *how much.* Her advance was little short of remarkable. The material might have been of the same kind as the first album, but there was a great deal more finesse in everything—from the writing, through the arrangements to the singing. She'd achieved exactly what she wanted, and fans saw that. The fact that its highest chart position was number 4 was immaterial. As a portrait of Mariah as an artist coming into bloom, it was everything anyone could hope for.

Walter Afanasieff thought it truly captured Mariah at that

time. "Her heart and soul is all over this record," he said, adding, "She's developed a wisdom and professionalism that goes beyond her twenty-one years"—a trait he attributed to her experience, which he felt lent her the focus that was apparent on this record. He was of the belief that "new pop singers are going to want to emulate Mariah."

As with the first album, Mariah was loathe to promote *Emotions* with public appearances. Except in one instance. She did perform on the 1991 MTV Video Music Awards. Onstage she came across relaxed and smiling, as if being there was second nature to her, quite a change from the year before when she'd complained of nervousness and shown no desire to play to live audiences. There was still no tour booked, but at least she'd made a small step in the right direction.

THE VIDEOS for the singles did eventually find commercial release, appended to the video of Mariah's "MTV Unplugged" show. The clips were preceded by an interview with Mariah (accompanied by her Doberman pinscher, Princess, and the cats Ninja and Thompkins), in which she talks about her experience in making the two albums back-to-back, which made them seem like one long album to her, and what she saw ahead for herself.

"Make It Happen" was directed by Marcus Nispel, who picked up on the gospel element of the song and used that as the focus of the concept, where Mariah performs her piece at a benefit to "Save Our Church." The audience, as they file into the dusty, deserted building, is made up of the widest cross section possible, old and young (with a strong emphasis on children), abled and disabled, all races and colors. Although they're here for a good cause, everyone is out to have fun. From the first beat dancers are moving. There's a deliberately amateurish, spontaneous air about things, from the old-fashioned square microphone (Mariah's prop in the ads for her first album, as well as in the "Vision of Love" video), to the small drum kit and beat-up piano. Editing cuts to faces on the growing crowd show people enjoying themselves, and a contented look on the face of the black minister, holding his young daughter (or granddaughter). The numbers onstage grow, too, as Mariah is joined by children playing cellos, and a group of black women singing backup. At the end, when the song finishes there are cheers—not on the record, but dubbed in to give more of a real, live experience to the video.

"Can't Let You Go," Jim Sonzero's first work with Mariah, is a beautifully lush piece of work, full of surprising and imaginative camera angles. Filmed in black-and-white, and in a muted focus, it's framed by its starting and finishing shots, first of a pair of clasped hands opening to reveal a white rose, then, at the end, closing over it again. Mariah is in the courtyard of a house, strongly lit to create large variances of light and shadow. Her hair up, wearing a short black dress, she sings as the lens cuts to images—flowers, a letter on a desk, the lines of a blind—over her words. Quite often the way the images are placed together make it difficult for a second or two to distinguish what is being filmed. And that's a good thing; it keeps the viewer's attention on the screen. For such a lonely song, it works well. This style had been attempted before, but rarely had it been done so well.

For "Emotions," director Jim Preiss honed in on the party element of the song and used that as his idea, reproduced here in the tune's "extended" version. The colors are toned down—blue for the interior scenes, brown (simulating firelight) for the evening fun outdoors, and even the daytime exteriors have a blurred, undefined edge to them.

The opening shots show Mariah, wearing a wrap over a fifties-style bikini, in the back of a convertible, singing as the couple in the front seat converses. From there, we cut to the party scenes, which take place at a large old house. Inside, people are dancing, looking through records and talking. A bush baby, someone's pet, wanders around lazily, big-eyed and curious. Outside, later, the party has heated up. Couples—black and white—dance and have fun. Notably, no one is shown drinking or using any kind of drugs, even tobacco. Throughout, Mariah is singing, to no one in particular, which emphasizes the sense of overall joy in the song. And, even more than on the record (although it's exactly the same track), the high notes work. They seem to punctuate the fun perfectly.

Then, at the very end of the tape, just before the credits, there is some home-movie footage of Mariah—running on the beach with Princess, swimming, signing autographs in a record store. Her voice runs over the pictures, thanking the fans who've helped her along the way with their support, letters. It's a simple gesture, but one most artists wouldn't ever think to make, and one that reinforces the idea that Mariah is truly a lady.

THIS SECOND ALBUM didn't bring out any more malicious gossip about Mariah being a white girl trying to sound black. It appeared as if the greater gospel and soul influences in her sound had managed to erase all that.

Unfortunately, one piece of gossip that Mariah had been unable to dispel was regarding her romance with Tommy Mottola. Although he'd long refuted it, and she'd more or less done the same ("I read that stuff and I throw it away"), the rumors continued. Mariah refused to talk about it; she would neither confirm nor deny anything. The closest she came to any kind of statement came in an interview with *USA Today,* when she was asked if she had a boyfriend and answered, "Sort of, but I'd rather not get into it."

Emotions ended a long, intense period of work for Mariah. Two years with virtually no break, a cycle of writing, recording, promoting, writing, recording, and promoting yet again, can leave a person exhausted. With the first record she had had to establish herself, make her name. That done—very, very successfully—on the second she had to show that *she* was at the heart of everything, and that she wasn't just another good singer who allowed herself to be shaped by her producers and her material. And *Emotions* certainly proved that. In taking full responsibility for the record, Mariah took on a challenge which she more than met head-on. She could write and sing in a variety of styles, she'd fully absorbed her influences, and she wasn't afraid to try and expand her musical range (as on "The Wind"). *Mariah Carey* was the record of a girl making herself known; *Emotions* was the sound of that young girl quickly reaching the start of maturation as an artist. (*Emotions* did garner one Grammy nomination, a joint one for Mariah and Walter Afanasieff as producers. But, at the 1992 ceremony it failed to win.)

More than that, she'd managed it with both style and dignity, and without hogging the spotlight. Other artists courted the crowds, and treated controversy like a close friend. Mariah wasn't one of them. Yes, she made videos, and was featured in them, but that was virtually an extension of making records. In reality she was more than happy to let the music speak for itself, and would very likely have been content to leave it at that, and never have to make another public singing appearance.

And so Mariah reached the end of one era. She'd grown tremendously, both artistically and personally, and had gone, almost before our eyes, from a girl to a woman, one who was both lovely and talented. Even if she never released another album, she'd made her mark, and would have a lasting place in the record books for her string of number 1 hits. But Mariah liked to stare challenges in the face, and the next one was just around the corner.

5

The source of the next problem in Mariah's life was perhaps unexpected—her family. To be specific, her stepfather, Joseph Vian—who'd married Patricia Carey in 1987, just before Mariah left home to seek her fame and fortune in Manhattan.

By early 1992 Vian and Patricia had split up and begun divorce proceedings that would become final later in the year. Meanwhile, however, Vian had begun proceedings against Mariah in Federal District Court in New York. He charged that Mariah "agreed orally that he would have a license to market singing dolls in her likeness," as well as other claims, including one that indicated that Mariah "was unjustly enriched at his expense in that he contributed to her support and to the development of her professional career, with the expectation of reward." This ran entirely counter to the way Mariah had previously told the story—that her mother would have bought her another pair of shoes to replace those holey sneakers she lived in for a year, but she preferred to be self-supporting. But perhaps the harshest blow here was his allegation that Mariah "intentionally and/or negligently . . . interfered in his relationship with his wife, defendant's mother, destroying that relationship and causing him to fall into a deep depression from which he has not recovered."

Whether Mariah liked Vian or not, the closeness of her relationship with her mother has been well shown and was never in doubt; it seems very unlikely that she would do anything to bring unhappiness to Patricia—on the contrary, she'd be far more likely to do what she could to make her mother happier. The Federal District Court judge obviously agreed, because later in the year he dismissed both that claim and others, including the allegation regarding Mariah unjustly enriching herself at Vian's expense.

Regarding the "Mariah dolls," that would take nearly a year to be settled, until April 1993 when Judge Michael B. Mukasey dismissed the charge, and stated, "In sum, [Vian] has not raised a triable issue of fact as to the existence of a contract." (Mariah, testifying by deposition, explained, regarding Vian's comments about the dolls, that she thought it was a joke.) The judge continued, "Viewing the facts in light most favorable to [Vian], as I have done in deciding this motion, there is no evidence that [Mariah] thought, or should have thought, that [he] was serious about entering into a contract, nor that she believed she had bound herself to a licensing agreement for 'Mariah dolls' by saying 'Okay' and nodding her head when her stepfather made passing references to the idea. . . ." and eventually concluded, "Even if the plaintiff had a valid contract, which I stress again he did not, he has not alleged recoverable damages." In essence, this was a reprimand for Vian, who was going away with nothing—except bad feelings, and, of course, none of the money that Mariah had made by her own talent.

THE BREAK that Mariah took from music proved to be very short, as might be expected from such a workaholic personality. She knew she needed to take her songs to the fans. After all, they'd bought literally millions of her albums and singles. But, as she'd said, she didn't want to undertake a concert tour. The solution came in the form of a television program.

MTV's "Unplugged" had been on the air for a few years before it became popular. Originally hosted by singer/songwriter Jules Shear ("If She Knew What She Wants"), it had been intended to provide an informal, live setting for musicians to offer very basic versions of their songs and sit in with other artists. That particular idea didn't seem to draw an audience, however, and the concept was revamped. Shear was dropped, and a greater concentration was placed on bringing in "name" artists, who would in turn attract more viewers. The idea proved phenomenally successful. Suddenly the idea of playing "unplugged" was everywhere—not only on television, but also in clubs. However, it wasn't as stripped down as the name implied. Whole bands appeared, and it was common to see drum kits and keyboards on the stage, with the groups just performing straight "acoustic" versions of their hits. Some, like LL Cool J, were more adventurous, offering rap freed from its samples and electric backdrop. But most, like Eric Clapton, were content to take the easy route, which ended up more bland than basic.

For Mariah, the "Unplugged" show was an ideal option. She would be seen by large numbers of people with cable TV—not only fans, but also the curious. By performing live she would be able to dispel any ideas of her being a "manufactured" artist. And, most importantly, working in this form would offer her a challenge, something she could never resist. On record, most of the instrumental backing for Mariah's voice had been provided by synthesizers and drum machines. An acoustic setting would require working with real musicians and singers; how could she turn it down?

The answer, obviously, was that she couldn't. And she didn't.

THE PROBLEMS she and Walter Afanasieff (by now her co-arranger of choice) faced were twofold. Firstly, what material should they pick? And then, how would they present it?

The big hits were what most people were familiar with, the songs they'd heard on the radio, with infectious choruses they could sing in their sleep. On the other hand, less familiar material, like, say, "Vanishing" and "The Wind" had great possibilities for such a show. In the end they decided to go with the popular tunes. It was a decision that made perfect sense for Mariah's big television debut (yes, she'd been on

"Saturday Night Live" and "Arsenio Hall," but this would be *her* show); it would be giving people what they really wanted to hear.

As for the presentation, that raised a number of possibilities. Straight renditions of the songs with acoustic instruments would probably be fine, and satisfy the public. But there was no real challenge in that. It didn't do anything new. Instead, Mariah fell back on her old loves, gospel and soul music, and decided to play it from those angles. While the rumors of "another white girl singing black" seemed to have died down with the release of *Emotions*, this would banish them completely.

Making preparations for the taping was a time-consuming venture. There was a great deal to be done before any rehearsals could be undertaken. Using real musicians as opposed to electronics necessitated bringing in both a string and a brass section, as well as piano, guitars, drums, and backing singers. Parts had to be written for all these people, and, with the emphasis on Mariah's gospel and soul side, these couldn't just duplicate the arrangements on the albums.

Once all that was done came the rehearsals, a difficult proposition with so many people, even if they were all top-notch musicians.

And finally, everything had to be sorted out in the studio. The idea of the program might be to be unplugged, but the reality involved a large number of microphones, a very carefully mixed sound, camera angles to be worked out, stage positions for all the performers. Plus there was Mariah's often-stated goal of perfection in everything. Which meant that the show's production crew had a nightmare. Luckily some of the technical staff were people who'd worked with her before. The mixing was handled by Dana Jon Chappelle, who'd handled exactly that job on both her albums, and the show's director was Larry Jordan, who had performed the same job on the "Someday" video. All in all, a crew of ten was needed to record the show.

But that wasn't all. ". . . [P]eople kept saying to do an

oldie," Mariah said. "Two nights before the actual show I decided on 'I'll Be There' " (a number 1 hit for the Jackson Five in 1970 which stayed at the top of the charts for five weeks). Which of course only added to the problems. Another song to arrange and learn, and to cause the crew headaches.

The taping took place before an invited audience at the Kaufman Astoria Studios in New York on March 16, 1992, eleven days before Mariah's twenty-second birthday.

The audience was ready for her, that was quite obvious from the cheers that greeted Mariah as she opened her mouth to sing the first notes of "Emotions." Dressed all in black—as was virtually everyone crowded onto the stage—in a short jacket, leotard, tight jeans, and boots—she was also ready for them.

As any fan might have predicted, it was a gospelish introduction. Guest David Cole, sitting in on piano (and the only one not completely in black; he wore a sparkling silver jacket) held the chords behind the voices, letting it all build, before the beat kicked in and everyone got to work.

Mariah had a small triangle of stage to herself, nearest the crowd. Everyone else was cramped. A four-piece string section sat off to the side (Belinda Whitney Barnett, Cecilia Hobbs-Gardner, Wince Garvey, and Laura Corcos) in front of Dan Shea, who'd worked out the string arrangements and was playing the harpsichord and harmonium. The rhythm section held the back of the stage—Gigi Conaway on drums, Randy Jackson on bass, Vernon Black on guitar, and two percussionists, Sammy Figueroa and Ren Klyce, who contributed timpanis, celeste, and tubular and orchestral bells. The other side of the stage was reserved for the "Saturday Night Live" horns (Lew Delgatto, baritone saxophone; Lenny Pickett, tenor saxophone; George Young, alto saxophone; Earl Gardner, trumpet; and Steve Turre, trombone), who would appear on one song.

In the past Mariah had referred to her music as "vocally driven," and the number of backup singers she surrounded herself with here really proved she meant it. There were ten of them clustered around the piano. Quite naturally, they were led by her longtime associates Trey Lorenz and Patrique McMillan, with the addition of Geno Morris and the Darryl Douglass Workshop Company (Kelly Price, Cheree Price, Melanie Daniels, Peggy Harley, Liz Stewart, Spencer Washington, and Henry Casper). By the first chorus of the opening song they'd proved their worth. They added the warmth of a Baptist church choir, weaving in and out behind Mariah's voice, and working with it to create the melody over the rhythm. In this context "Emotions," though the same tune and the same words, sounded quite different—much rawer and earthier, two qualities Mariah had wanted in her music from the time of her debut record. David Cole had the right touch, adding notes and fills that accentuated the feel. Mariah touched her high notes perfectly, and when the instruments cut out before the song's end, leaving just the voices, it seemed perfect. Many in the studio would probably have been quite content to have had a whole show of just voices!

The audience had been clapping along with the beat from the start, and would do so for all the uptempo material. One small, particularly active group was dancing and waving behind the stage.

It all felt right, as if this was the perfect way to see Mariah Carey. If she appeared nervous at first, standing by the microphone, she overcame it very quickly, walking around, singing to the crowd and the camera. As the song ended, and the applause began, she giggled. Only she knew what reaction she'd been expecting, but this outpouring seemed to surprise and gratify her. There were still some nerves in her, of course—that was only to be expected, and she expressed them as giggles—but she definitely truly appreciated these fans, thanking them after every piece, and their reception helped her slowly relax over the course of the taping.

After the first song "the incredible" Walter Afanasieff replaced David Cole at the piano, and the "Saturday Night Live" horns took the stage to perform the tune Mariah had written with "one of my idols"—Carole King. The recorded version had a Southern soul feel—the kind that filled material that came out on the Stax label in the late sixties—which really mixed soul and gospel, but this version truly captured that idea. And with the additional voices, it could almost have been recorded in church.

This made it quite clear that not only had Mariah and Walter (who co-arranged the material for this show) "broke[n] the arrangements down to their simplest forms by using only acoustic instruments," they'd in fact done much more. This style perfectly suited both Mariah's voice and her songs, and the interaction with other musicians, as opposed to synthesizers, added a warmth to the music that made it more immediate and alive.

"If It's Over," with its lazy rhythm and stop-time pause beats served Mariah's lower register well, although on the vocal "breakdown" at the crescendo she couldn't resist letting the octaves soar briefly skyward.

However, it was impossible not to note the stylistic differences at the keyboard between Walter Afanasieff and David Cole. Cole was much freer in his playing, just concentrating on that, while Walter's style was more formal, and he also had to lead an entire band of twenty-six, who looked to him for their musical cues. For the specifically gospel-style performance Mariah was giving, Cole (or someone like him) was a much more suitable performer. That's not to take away from Afanasieff's talent (maybe even genius) by any means; his gift is obvious, and his empathy with Mariah has worked very well for both of them. And, for ballads, he has an ideal style, subdued, playing to the voice rather than around it. But this particular type of live performance needed a more outgoing style, one which led rather than followed.

This really showed on the next song, "Someday." Cole's churchy stylings could have added a great deal to it. Not that it was a bad version; not by any means. It percolated well, with the voices bouncing over the rhythm section. And it gave Mariah a real chance to show off her vocal gymnastics. But the spark that would have turned something good into something really special never quite ignited. However, for the audience it was just fine, very happily caught up in the moment, clapping to the beat. And even Mariah herself seemed happy with it, turning to exchange smiles with the others.

That was, Mariah said when it was over, the last time she would be needing to use the top end of her range for the evening, for which she seemed quite glad, although she'd been sparing with it so far, making it a necessary part of the songs, rather than a twist or a gimmick. Noticeably, live, to be able to hear herself in that area, she needed to block one ear with a hand or finger. That technique, common among folk singers, enables the singer to get an accurate gauge of pitch, from which one can only assume that all the sophisticated electronics used on the show, including the monitors (small speakers facing the performers which allow them to hear everybody else onstage) didn't do a very good job of broadcasting frequencies that high.

When things slowed a little for what to many was still Mariah's "big hit," "Vision of Love," she had a chance to perch on a stool. For such an inexperienced live performer, she'd held control of the audience remarkably well, and this immediately recognizable piece was the last step necessary to cement that bond.

Again, with all the other voices to play off of, and with its swaying, lulling rhythm, it came across as quite fresh, without the Top 40 gloss that had characterized the single. As with all her material, such rawness suited it, giving it a kick of emotion and, once more, a gospelish edge that pointed out the hopefulness of the lyrics. And, by sticking with her lower register, Mariah was able to offer a throatier performance. (Interestingly, as she's moved further from her debut, with its high notes which helped to initially make her name known, Mariah has kept more and more to her lower register, which allows her singing technique, rather than any ornament, to shine.)

For "Make It Happen" David Cole returned to the stage, to duet with Walter Afanasieff on the piano. He took the right-hand, or treble, parts, with Walter supplying the underpinning, or bass parts. Cole's energy was quite infectious, his big smile shining as much as any of the stage lights, bouncing to the beat on the piano stool. This pairing illustrated perfectly the point raised earlier about the difference in the two mens' styles. Cole brought the song alive, filling in with little runs, working against the beat on the chorus, giving it the fire that "Some-day" never quite managed, even animating Walter to move with him. His innate feel for this kind of music shone through in his playing. It might have been simple, but every note was effective.

All the vocalists obviously caught this too, for they sang just like a church choir ("Make It Happen" was, in its own way, a song of praise), letting the repeated choruses build be-hind Mariah, giving her a chance to wail and solo, not like any pop diva performing for a crowd, but someone filled with the spirit. The roughness of this version succeeded in a way the recorded version on *Emotions* could never manage. In the sterile atmosphere of a studio, where perfection, technology, and overdubbing were the rules, spontaneity had no real place. On the stage it was valued, and this had it. Everyone pushed ev-eryone else a little further, to create something wonderful, and, judging by their response, the audience realized it, as did Mariah when it finished. It was a rare moment, one that true performers strive for and don't find often enough to satisfy themselves.

It was followed by another rare moment, the hastily as-sembled adaptation of the Jackson Five's "I'll Be There." The way Walter and Mariah had arranged the song, she took the Michael Jackson lead, and Trey Lorenz, with his high, sweet voice, took what had originally been Jermaine Jackson's part, the second lead. After two years of working with Mariah, he was getting his chance to shine, and, outfitted in a worn black leather motorcycle jacket and baseball cap, he looked ready for it.

It was interesting that, with so many songs of her own, Mariah chose to cover a tune that was more than twenty years old. As a bit of fun, or as a tribute to that band, it was a good idea. But almost certainly no one could have predicted the impact this particular performance would have. As good as everything so far had been—and it had been exceptional—suddenly giving Maria a reputation as a live performer that would have been difficult for anyone, let alone a rookie, to live up to; this propelled it into the stratosphere.

On the surface there was nothing remarkable about it. The song had been covered many times over the years, by any number of people. But maybe it was the friendship between Mariah and Trey, or maybe it was the atmosphere that was in the studio that night. Whatever the cause, it brought out something amazing in both singers and started Trey Lorenz on a well-earned solo career.

With such a short preparation time, the instrumental arrangement was very basic, just a simple backing for the voices, all of which back Mariah on her verses. When she introduced Trey for his part, he seemed bashful at first, then he dove into the role and sang his heart out. The first time around he stuck to the melody, giving a beautiful counterpoint to Mariah's alto. But, on his second chance, he climaxed by soaring into the high, unbelievable falsetto that had first made Mariah take notice of him in the studio. It was another of those perfect moments, and everyone realized it, performers and audience alike. Mariah seemed quite content to hold back (although her performance was equally lovely and tender) and let Trey bask in the spotlight.

Later he would be unable to recall his performance, which he didn't hear for a few months after the taping: ". . . [G]reat goodness, I *think* we were singing really good that day, but I wasn't so sure about me. I was really relieved when I listened."

All too often today, concerts bring standing ovations followed by planned encores. Mariah and Trey's rendition of "I'll Be There" literally brought the crowd out of their seats, clapping and cheering, an accolade that was honestly earned. After that, almost anything would have come as something of an anticlimax. So the show ended on a low-key note, with "Can't Let Go," which saw Mariah backed only by piano, percussion, bass, and voices. It was, she insisted, an off-the-cuff performance of the song, the arrangement made up as they went along, but it seems likely there was at least *some* rehearsal, however perfunctory, for it to work that well.

This really was a song stripped to its basics, quite raw, which only served to increase its appeal. The lyrics, which were full of heartbreak and confusion, truly came across (a tribute to Mariah's vocal ability) with complete vulnerability, and her swoop through the upper register just before the song's close gave it a wonderful, if unexpected, conclusion.

Needless to say, the crowd, which had been utterly won over from the beginning, was ecstatic. Mariah herself, to judge from her grin, was pleased with the way things had gone. A show, particularly one with so many musicians, involved a great deal of rehearsal, and the sessions for this had gone quickly and been intense. She was lucky in that a number of the participants had worked with her on her albums and were therefore familiar with much of the material. And the rest were experienced session musicians. But even then, mistakes can happen. For this, though, none did; in fact, things couldn't have gone any better if they'd been planned that way.

It was also a learning experience for Mariah: " 'Unplugged' taught me a lot about myself because I tend to nitpick everything I do and make it a little too perfect because I'm a perfectionist," she told *Billboard*'s Melinda Newman. "I'll always go over the raw stuff and now I've gotten to the point where I understand that the raw stuff is usually better."

Originally Mariah's "Unplugged" show was meant to simply be a telecast, to stand or fall on its own. It would air on MTV and that would be the end of things. No video, and most certainly no album—after all, *Emotions* was still doing well, having gone multi-platinum, and since the show was short and contained no real new material, there seemed to be no point in releasing it. Besides, Mariah and Walter were already hard at work, beginning to write songs for her third album, scheduled to appear sometime during 1993.

But public reaction has a power all its own, as has been shown by the way *Mariah Carey* and the singles from it sold, far beyond the possibilities or dreams of any record-company hype.

MTV usually aired each new "Unplugged" show a few times over the course of a month, then retired it to the vaults, to be dragged out and dusted off every once in a while. From the first time it was shown, though, Mariah's show proved almost unbelievably popular. Calls came in from all over the country, causing far more reruns of the performance than had been anticipated. Nor was it only popular with fans; critics, too, found much to praise in it. *Time*'s Christopher John Farley called it "deservedly acclaimed," and his words only echoed sentiment around the country. Upon the release of the show as an EP (an abbreviation for "extended play"—a format which was very popular in the sixties, consisting of four tracks on a 7" vinyl disc, but which had since fallen out of favor), *Rolling Stone* reviewed it with Eric Clapton's MTV set, saying that her version of "I'll Be There" could easily be mistaken for the Jackson Five's, "and that's a mighty compliment." The reviewer was also enthusiastic about "Someday," "transformed into a bubbly gush of pure pop," and ended, "Carey bests Clapton in a battle of the bands? Only on MTV."

The groundswell was such that Columbia was more or less forced to issue the show. People wanted it to play at home, in their cars, wherever. And, more than anything, they wanted to listen to the version of "I'll Be There." So that was what the company gave them. *MTV Unplugged* came out as a reduced-price EP, because of its shorter length, and "I'll Be There" was released as a single.

Both were remarkably successful. "I'll Be There" debuted on the Hot 100 at number 13, the highest entry yet for one of Mariah's songs. Probably not even Mariah could have dreamed that it would do so well, nor could she have imagined that such a hastily chosen and rehearsed cover song would give her a sixth number 1 hit. But it did, barely pausing on its way to the top of the charts. After four weeks it was in the number 1 spot, after brief pauses at number 4 and number 2, and it stayed there for two weeks beginning June 20, 1992.

The EP debuted on the album charts the week the single reached number 1, coming in at number 8. The next week it rose to number 5, and peaked at number 3. Not as good a performance as "I'll Be There," it was still far more than credible for a piece of work which wasn't even originally going to be released, particularly given the fact that it would go on to sell more than 2 million copies.

It's certainly worth noting that Mariah and Columbia Records decided to donate part of the proceeds from the *MTV Unplugged* EP to a number of charities: AmFAR (the American Foundation for AIDS Research), the United Negro College Fund, Hale House Center, Inc., and the T. J. Martell Foundation, another AIDS-related organization. It seemed only right; after all, they'd had a hit record given to them from something they'd never intended to release. But, still, it was a magnanimous gesture, and one that was rightly done with a minimum of publicity.

THIS SUCCESS had a gratifying side effect. It gave Trey Lorenz a solo career. Epic (part of the Columbia family of labels and one-time home of Brenda K. Starr) signed him, not just on the strength of that one song, but also the other work he'd done with Mariah, and his own ability. Suddenly the important thing was for him to get a good record out as soon as possible, before his name was forgotten.

It turned out that he had the best possible help. Mariah and Walter were looking ahead to her new album but, she said, "I really didn't want all the fun and interest behind him with the 'I'll Be There' record to go to waste, so we just went at it for about three months." And what had been a writing session for Mariah "became a Trey writing session instead. . . . I was really into the project."

In fact she was so into it that she chose to produce, or co-produce six tracks on his album. On five of those she worked with Walter Afanasieff. Nor were they the only star talents employed in the production booth. There was Keith Thomas, who had worked with both Amy Grant and Vanessa Williams, Mark C. Rooney, Mark Morales, Glen Ballard and BeBe Winans, part of the gospel group the Winans.

Mariah's involvement extended to cowriting two of the songs, which proved to be the most difficult for her to produce. "I'm sort of writing them as we go along," she said. "When you don't have a demo to refer to and you're doing the track, it's like, 'What am I going to sing on this line and how should the background go on this one?' as opposed to when someone else has already written it and you just do it."

Quite naturally, the arrangements centered around Trey's vocals, with many of the vocal arrangements and backgrounds handled by Mariah, as well as Will Downing, Audrey Wheeler, and Cindy Mizelle (who had already established a relationship with Mariah by appearing on *Emotions*). And the production experience triggered some ideas in Mariah of perhaps producing others ("possibly a contemporary gospel [artist]"), although no names were mentioned, nor any time—and to date it hasn't happened, although it well might in the future.

However, this was *Trey's* big break; Mariah's involvement was important, both to it having happened in the first place and to its future success, but in the end it really all came down to him, and the work he'd put in over the years. His musical career hadn't begun with Mariah—very far from it. In fact, he'd been involved with music for most of his life, singing in church in Florence, South Carolina, with his parents, then taking piano lessons, before joining the Players, a Top 40 band, on vocals and keyboards, and having a brief fling with a group called Squeak and the Deep while majoring in advertising at Fairleigh Dickinson University.

Trey Lorenz was preceded by a single, "Someone to Hold." If it didn't have quite the impact on the charts that Mariah's first single had, it still sold more than respectably, climbing through chart positions in the thirties all the way to the teens before falling again. Not at all bad for a former backup singer! Its success certainly helped pull the album along on its release, giving it a chance to crack the Top Fifty on the charts.

Mariah took a great deal of pride in her protégé's acceptance by the record-buying public. "I'm trying not to talk too much and let the music speak for itself, but I think people are ready to hear him." And obviously they were, from the way his solo career was launched. Having pushed him out of the nest and seen him fly, though, Mariah didn't end her involvement with him. Trey didn't sing on the *Music Box* album, but he did sing on her television special, and opened the concert she performed as part of her tour on December 2, 1993, at the Spectrum in Philadelphia, giving *him* the chance to perform live before a large group of people.

OF COURSE, having now released the EP, that couldn't be the sum total of Columbia's effort with Mariah's "Unplugged" show. With large numbers of people—and Mariah Carey fans—throughout the country having no access to cable television, there was a very definite market for a video of the show and, to forestall any possible bootlegging, Sony Music Video released it under the title *"MTV Unplugged"* + 3. Given that the performance itself ran only half an hour long, they added the three videos from *Emotions*, which hadn't seen any previous commercial release, some backstage footage of Mariah rehearsing and performing on "Soul Train," a short interview, and some black-and-white "home movie" footage of Mariah frolicking on the beach with her dog Princess. Put together that way, it made a very nice package, a present for fans and new converts alike. Those who'd come to her music through the "Unplugged" show were given a sampling of album material to contrast the rawness of the live experience with studio polish.

The most important aspect of the "Unplugged" show wasn't the record and video sales it ended up generating, but the fact that it proved Mariah to be an extremely valid live performer, and one who had a very sure sense of whatever direction she wanted her live show to take, at that. Whenever she finally did decide to tour—which at this point was still not even being considered—she would be able to undertake the venture with a great deal more confidence. And while she might not be able to recreate the close feeling of her "Unplugged" show—when she toured she would undoubtedly be playing stadiums and large theaters, while the style she'd used on the show depended on its intimacy and the subtlety of vocal interplay for much of its impact—she had quite firmly shown what she was capable of doing.

But, far more than that, it put her in control of her own music. Not that she wasn't before, at least to some extent. After all, it would be difficult not to have some control when you're the singer, cocomposer, co-arranger, and coproducer. By this time, though, she'd found her audience and established herself with a very strong fan base, and she could afford to indulge *her* tastes a little, which is the feeling that comes across in the "Unplugged" show—that its direction originates very much with Mariah. On her first album she'd taken suggestions from Columbia (albeit grudgingly on occasion, having firm ideas of the way she wanted it to sound), admitting that it was their money. *Emotions* had more of her in every part of it, but it was only a stop on the road to "Unplugged," her proving ground.

How much influence this performance would carry on her next record would be seen in the future. The fact that public demand caused the release of *Unplugged* as an EP, and the commercial success of such a project, would suggest that her ideas carry a great deal of weight. Much would depend on the type of songs she and Walter had been writing, which no one knew yet. Another factor to be considered was her production work for Trey Lorenz, which opened her eyes to a large number of studio possibilities.

But all of that lay in the future. Mariah was certainly due a good rest by now, away from the grind of recording and promotion. For three and a half years that had been her life, day in and day out, and while it had documented her remarkable growth as an artist, even an artist can burn out. Besides, it had given Mariah very little time to enjoy any kind of life of her own, and while she might have dreamed about music when other girls dreamed of marriage, those dreams had been more than adequately filled by now, not only as a performer and songwriter, but finally as a producer of someone else.

The writing for the next album would continue, of course. For Mariah, it would be impossible for her to stop doing that. This, after all, is a woman who has stated that she will call her answering service to hum a line for a new song or note a fragment of a lyric. But at least the whole—writing, recording, mixing of the record—could be taken at a more relaxed, more *sensible* pace after the breakneck speed she'd been keeping up.

And having given her fans a great deal of product over the last three years, Mariah could afford to take a year or more between albums without it seeming as if she'd ever been away. She was still one of the (if not *the*) leading pop divas, and there were no newcomers on the horizon, no pretenders to the throne waiting around the corner. It remained, as it had been

Smile for the camera. That's great!

Reflecting on the new life

The joy of success

*On tour—Mariah at
Madison Square
Garden*

Giving it all to the music

Always a commanding presence on stage

Triumphing at the 1991 MTV Video Music Awards

Two more for the awards shelf

*Out on the town—
Mr. and Mrs. Mottola*

Just married: Mariah and Tommy Mottola on the big day

in 1990 when *Mariah Carey* was released, Mariah and Whitney.

SUCH WAS THE NATURE of mainstream pop music in the nineties; it was more or less static. The same few names tended to crop up again and again—Mariah, Whitney, Phil Collins, Billy Joel, and a few others. These were the artists who would be perennially popular, not only with the young, but with all age groups. What had changed was the huge public acceptance of both rap and alternative music. The impact they'd made was felt not only in the album charts, an area one might expect, but also in the Hot 100. Rap acts were making the Top Twenty with astonishing regularity. Rap fashions became the norm for a whole set of teenagers, while another set, inspired by the whole "Seattle sound" (which proved to be the catalyst that ignited the popularity of "alternative music") settled into the plaid flannel and torn jeans of grunge chic.

Neither would affect Mariah's record sales. A Mariah Carey fan would be unlikely to be interested in the latest Nirvana record, and vice versa. And, unlike Whitney Houston— whose records, interestingly, suddenly seemed to be more heavily weighted toward ballads—Mariah's dance material owed far more to soul and disco than any current hip-hop trend. Paying less attention to fads would yield another long-term dividend, although she may not have realized it: her songs wouldn't sound out of date anywhere near as fast. Rather, they would have that timeless quality that seemed to be the property of the very best of singers—the Streisands, Sinatras, and Holidays—no bad thing in itself, and a big asset to a young singer with many productive years ahead of her. And they were definitely appreciated by the public, who, in February 1993, added to her awards shelf two American Music Awards (which had the added effect of boosting her sales—the

Unplugged EP rising back to number 44 from number 71 the week after she hoisted the trophies for the cameras).

IN HER HIGH SCHOOL YEARBOOK, Mariah had listed her interests as sleeping late, Corvettes, and "guiedos" (sic). Well, these days she could afford a new (or vintage, for that matter) Corvette for every day of the month, if not the year, and she could sleep until whatever time she chose, with no one to tell her she was being lazy, throw off the covers, and get her out of bed.

Which left one thing.

From the beginning of her climb to superstardom Mariah had been very reluctant to talk about any romance in her life, to the point of secrecy. It wasn't part of the business, and that made it hers and hers alone. All the rumors that circulated about her and Tommy Mottola (of Italian descent), she dismissed out of hand.

But it wouldn't be long before the whole world had a chance to learn what was going on in Mariah's private life, and to share her joy in it.

6

"A lot of young women get disillusioned looking for Mr. Right. He never shows up in most cases. But in my case, yes!"

That was the way Mariah talked about her romance and upcoming marriage, when she finally was willing to open up about it. Actually, it wasn't even really a case of being willing to open up about it. It was rather that she couldn't keep it a secret any longer, not after a wedding date had been set and all the arrangements had been set in motion.

So who was the lucky man?

Tommy Mottola.

Despite all their denials, the rumors had continued, even if they'd died down somewhat after the *Emotions* album. In all fairness, they'd been incredibly discreet. No pictures had been published in any tabloid papers of the two of them together, nothing that might even begin to tarnish the reputation of either one. Tommy was divorced, his settlement final after a fairly bitter court fight in 1991. And Mariah had had no previous ties. There were a few reports of boyfriends in the past, but nothing serious or more than a high school type of romance. This, on the other hand, was quite definitely the real thing.

Not too surprisingly, the beginnings of this love match had happened after Tommy signed her to Columbia. At first everything was completely businesslike, but that changed over the time she was making *Mariah Carey* (during which period Tommy separated from his wife). "It just sort of happened," Mariah said. "We had a lot in common, and we just gradually came together."

The need for secrecy was obvious. He was the head of her record company, quite possibly the most influential single record executive in America at the time. He had discovered her, brought her to Columbia, and for all intents and purposes he had been her mentor, guiding her career—at least in the beginning. On *Mariah Carey* and *Emotions* he had received executive-producer credit. If their burgeoning romance had truly become public, things would have been a little difficult for Tommy Mottola; the way he had been pushing her could easily have been viewed as a case of conflict of interest. And, with his separation and divorce so recent, Mariah might well have ended up being tagged "the other woman," which may seem outdated these days, but it still carries a large stigma with a lot of people.

There was one other factor that made the pairing seem strange. Tommy was almost twenty years older than Mariah. While there have been many successful, happy unions with such an age gap, it remains unusual. However, Mariah said, "I don't focus on it. We don't look at each other with a big age difference. We are just right for each other, and that is all that matters. If you are really right for each other, that will shine through all the differences, everything—race and age." And, she added, "I don't think of Tommy as an older person. I think of him as a very special person. Everybody who knows us realizes that we're right for each other."

But it still seemed odd. Mariah, so young and bouncy, with so much living to do, a vegetarian with very strong professed views about her independence. And Mottola, whose daily life was consumed by business matters, a collector of guns and a hunter. There were so many opposites. Still, as the old saying goes, love conquers all, and it apparently had done so in this case.

"Tommy is just the greatest person," Mariah told Steve Dougherty in *People* magazine. "He knows so much; he's funny. I can't imagine anybody else who would be so supportive and so understanding and helpful. He lifts me up." They were indisputably the words of a woman in love.

Even so, the fact that she was actually going to get married, to make such a huge commitment, seemed to surprise Mariah. "I never thought I would [get married] because my parents got divorced, and it gives you a different attitude about that sort of thing. It kind of hardens you; you know what I mean?" It was quite understandable. She'd seen the bad side. She had the deep memories of the fights, the tears, the pain, and she knew what it was like to grow up in what used to be called "a broken home." It would be enough to make anyone think twice about taking such a big step. Later Mariah would admit that her friends were equally surprised by her move, half expecting her to have an attack of cold feet before it happened: ". . . [E]verybody that knows me was freaked out that I actually did it. I think they thought I was going to run at the last minute."

But while preparations for her big day took up more and more of Mariah's time, they didn't fill it completely. There was still the small matter of her career. During 1992 and the early part of 1993, crammed in among her other obligations, Mariah and Walter Afanasieff (and others) had written the material for her next album, and she'd recorded it, using what had become her favorite studio for vocals, Right Track in New York, a place where she could just lose herself singing. "I love to go in and sing all the background parts and then hear like twenty tracks of my own voice coming back out of the speaker," she said, describing the place where she felt happiest. By spring the project had been completed, ready for release in the late summer or early fall, one of Columbia's big albums of the season, which would lead into Christmas and generate plenty of extra sales. After the fairly relaxed time of this record, things began getting hectic again as the wedding date grew closer. As with almost every wedding in history, it was a case of "so much to do, so little time."

* * *

TRADITIONALLY, JUNE IS THE MONTH when brides walk down the aisle, and since Mariah has a wide streak of romanticism in her heart, she would be no exception. The couple named the day to the press and Mariah's fans; it would be June 5, 1993, a Saturday. But that would only be the end of things. Before the ceremony and reception, there was the service to plan—it would be a church wedding, in line with Mariah's traditional approach to things—the invitations to be sent, the gown and shoes to be designed, a never-ending list.

At least, in this modern age, Mariah was able to employ wedding consultants to take care of most of the work. Like every bride, she wanted her wedding to be special. Unlike most of them, though, she had the money (not to mention the name) to make sure it would be. To be certain the press wouldn't be able to spread all the details beforehand, some of the consultants, at least the ones dealing with what she would wear, had to sign four-page affidavits binding them to secrecy before they were employed.

Able to take her pick of designers, Mariah finally settled on Vera Wang, a well-known name in the fashion world who specializes in wedding dresses. The gown, it was decided, would be quite spectacular, befitting a young woman of her status.

What Mariah *really* wanted for a wedding was something based on Prince Charles and Princess Diana's 1981 ceremony. Never mind the way that marriage had ended up—the day itself, which had been a real triumph of pomp and circumstance, was enough to inspire her. It was, of course, romantic. But while London—indeed, the whole of England and a great deal of the world—had come to a standstill for that, it was unlikely that New York would grind to a halt, even for Mariah Carey and Tommy Mottola.

Still, she watched a tape of the proceedings "over and over," getting the flavor of it, and absorbing ideas. Given her attitude toward the wedding, it was a given that the dress would be traditional. Mariah obviously enjoyed wearing short dresses for her videos and live shows, but get married in one . . . never! It was something that Lady Di would never have dreamed of.

The gown was merely one indication that no expense would be spared to make Mariah's special day perfect. The services of a top designer don't come cheap, nor does that fabrication of a custom dress (and Wang's routinely sold for $25,000). The second indication was when Mariah ordered her wedding shoes, a pair of pumps from shoe designer Vanessa Noel, at a cost of $1,000.

Something old, something new, something borrowed, something blue. That's what they say brides should wear. Mariah had the "new" in her dress and her pumps. "Something old" would be the 1893 English sixpence she planned to wear inside one of the pumps. "Something borrowed" was a family heirloom, a tiara, which she had redesigned in an imitation of the one Diana had worn on her wedding day. And "something blue"? Well, it was never disclosed, but the usual thing is a garter. Whether that was the item we don't know, but surely a bride has a right to *some* secrets, even one as visible and popular as Mariah Carey.

In the meantime the other details were all falling into place. Given Tommy Mottola's position and influence in the record industry, the guest list looked as if it was going to read like a Who's Who of popular music. There was at least one person invited, though, who seemed unlikely to attend, since Mottola was overheard saying jokingly to Barbra Streisand, a good friend of the man concerned, that Mariah really wanted President Clinton at the church, and was there anything she could do about it? In the end, neither the chief executive nor his wife attended, and Mariah didn't appear *too* upset by their absence. But by then she probably had quite a few other things on her mind.

* * *

IN NEW YORK CITY, June 5, 1993, was a rainy day. Not the type of weather a bride would choose for her big day, but the weather was one thing beyond the control of even Tommy Mottola. And the dampness certainly didn't diminish Mariah's anticipation.

Nor did it lessen the excitement of a group of her fans who arrived early to wait outside St. Thomas Episcopal Church on Fifth Avenue. It wasn't a small group, either, the numbers rising through the morning until it reached several hundred, with reporters, photographers, and television news crews jostling to the front for a better view and better pictures. This was an important wedding, a celebrity occasion, and magazines and six-o'clock reports were all primed to give it coverage.

When Mariah arrived, she truly looked like the fairy-tale bride, like Cinderella about to marry the prince. Emerging from the limousine, she was wearing a gorgeous off-the-shoulder gown in pale ivory silk, its bodice beaded over the material. The veil that covered her face was ten feet long, made of English tulle sprinkled with rhinestones to sparkle in the light and the raindrops. As she began to walk up the steps to the church doors, the dress kept coming from the car, the train slowly gathered up by six "ladies in waiting" until it was revealed in its full glory—all twenty-seven feet of it! "It took so many people to shove that thing in there," she laughed later. "It was . . . a major ordeal."

As major ordeals go, she could have experienced much worse. Things went very smoothly. The church was packed with faces familiar to any casual observer of entertainment magazines. Barbra Streisand, Michael Bolton, Bruce Springsteen (one of the few men who didn't dress up in a tuxedo and black tie) with his wife Patti Scialfa, and Robert DeNiro, for whom the event was so important that he was willing to take a day's break from his directorial film debut, *A Bronx Tale*. Billy Joel and supermodel spouse Christie Brinkley; Latin pop star Gloria Estefan, fully recovered from her broken back; television sitcom star Tony Danza; actor William Baldwin, accompanied by girlfriend Chynna Phillips, formerly of the singing group Wilson Phillips; and, perhaps surprisingly, heavy-metal singer Ozzy Osbourne. Even veteran disc jockey and game-show host Dick Clark was in attendance as the couple said their vows. And with the presence of such talent—all in all there were about three hundred guests—there was naturally some security; quite a lot of it, in fact, with personnel numbering another two hundred.

Episcopalian services tend toward the plain and simple, not lasting too long (unlike a Catholic wedding, which can stretch out for two hours), so it wasn't a tedious wait for the guests before Tommy was slipping the six-carat, pear-shaped diamond wedding ring onto the third finger of Mariah's left hand, a suitable companion for the other diamond she wore on her right hand. Relatively speaking, given the size and obvious cost of the day, it was unostentatious, although its worth was never stated.

Then, as the groom kissed the bride, it was over. They turned to face the photographer and video cameraman and walked down the aisle as man and wife. Outside the church a limousine was waiting, but on the steps were the flower girls, forty-seven of them, waiting to shower the happy pair with rose petals. Then it was the gauntlet of fans and press before being able to drive away to the reception, a whole procession of limos en route for the exclusive Metropolitan Club, rented for the occasion.

The reception had the conventional tone of a wedding reception anywhere in the country, at least unless you looked at the guests. There was a catered buffet, offering grilled shrimp, pasta, baby chickens. A disc jockey played music—Tommy had chosen oldies, songs from the Motown era and further back, including the highly appropriate "Chapel of Love," by the Dixie Cups. Mariah preferred something only a little more recent, seventies disco. When the DJ wasn't working his turntables, an orchestra was on hand to provide music. Notably, none of Mariah's hits was performed, nor did any of the amazing talent on hand stand up to sing with the band.

Without any doubt at all, it was the most perfect day of Mariah's life, a bigger thrill than any number 1 hit or Grammy award could offer. "The whole thing was like a dream," she recalled later. "Tommy has a lot of friends who happen to be famous."

Mariah and Tommy stayed into the early evening, when it was time to depart for their honeymoon—like so many couples, they were going to Hawaii. Fans were still waiting, having moved from the church to the Metropolitan Club, and Mariah gave them a gift for their patience and devotion, tossing her bouquet into a waiting group. But inside, the party continued, celebrities dancing, eating, and having a chance to let their hair down together.

Later the cost of the whole day would be estimated at $500,000. That could be seen as sheer indulgence, a lot of money spent unnecessarily. It could also be looked at as something both the bride and groom could easily afford without the usual scrimping and saving a wedding demands, so why not? As Mariah said, "I used to think of marriage as the end of the road; but now I'm ready to make a commitment." Commitments are things that last; why shouldn't they—and particularly such a large one—be celebrated in style?

ON THEIR RETURN FROM HAWAII, the couple was able to divide their time between two homes, an apartment in Manhattan—a necessity for both of them, but particularly for Tommy, who needed to be in the city five days a week—and an estate in upstate New York, located in the Hudson River Valley. The house was a large, renovated colonial, expensively restored to perfect condition, with a number of acres of both woodland and mowed pasture for Mariah to indulge her passion for the outdoors, either in vehicles—a Jeep, an ATV (all-terrain vehicle, a four-wheel motorcycle)—or on one of the four horses in the barn, including Mariah's favorite palomino, Misty.

The horses were among the new additions to Mariah's menagerie. There were still Ninja and Thompkins and Princess, but they'd been joined by another Doberman pinscher and Jack, a Jack Russell terrier with a passion for water.

Near the two-story main house, which stands on a hill overlooking the property, is the guest lodge, ready for whoever might drop by. With the peace of nature all around, it's easy to believe that this bucolic paradise was a million miles from the music business, instead of the short ninety miles from New York where it's actually located.

Inside the decor is chic, expensive country, the two main rooms filled with comfortable couches and chairs, while saddles rest in seemingly odd places, on banisters and on the arms of chairs, ready to be carried out and used. And, of course, the place is filled with photographs of Mariah and of Tommy, and a videotape of their nuptials. The only thing missing is the wedding album, which they keep in the city.

Their life together seems quite relaxed and contented. There is only one realm where Mottola is the undisputed king—the kitchen. "Tommy is a wonderful cook," Mariah said happily. "I'm *so* spoiled by his cooking. I bake when I'm bored, but he's the chef." She's even given up her vegetarian ways to fully enjoy his cooking. And she is finally able to have that maid she'd joked about with Patricia when she was a teenager—a virtual necessity since, by her own admission, Mariah isn't much of a homemaker, and taking care of such a place is a full-time job.

With two such strong people, though, both involved in the same business, there are disagreements at times, particularly since Tommy is "very creative, more than just a businessman," but nothing that can't be ironed out over a good meal.

They've even already talked about having children, something they both want, but it will be "eventually, not too soon," she's explained.

* * *

IT WASN'T TOO LONG AFTER the marriage, in September 1993, that Tommy Mottola received a promotion at work. For five years he had headed Sony's American music division, consisting of Columbia, Epic, and associated labels. In that time he had seen Columbia return to an ascendent position in the country, which it had lost in the few years before to WEA (Warner Elektra Asylum). Not only had Mottola's big names (Billy Joel, Barbra Streisand, Michael Jackson) all sold very well, but under Tommy's leadership a large number of new acts had been taken on board. Some sold remarkably from the beginning, like Pearl Jam and Alice in Chains. Others, like the Spin Doctors, had required some development, which the label was willing to offer. Sony had also widened its musical net to take in rap acts like Cypress Hill, whose sales proved the decision to be a wise one, and neo-folk groups like the Indigo Girls, a critically appreciated band who had come up through independent labels and have ended up with large worldwide sales and sold-out concert dates around the globe.

And then, of course, there was Mottola's new wife, Mariah Carey. The sales of her two albums and *Unplugged* EP more than justified the leap of faith Mottola had taken, not just in signing her, but in the money spent on the promotional campaign for her first record, something which had at times been criticized by people within the company. Her success was not only domestic, but global, throughout Europe, Australia, and Asia.

The jump in record sales that boosted Sony's position wasn't Mottola's only achievement within the company, however. With his background in so many areas of the music business, he helped the company rebuild its music-publishing division, which had been allowed to lapse, but had been a strong, ongoing source of income. He'd also set up a joint venture with an outside entrepreneur to develop and operate outdoor concert venues. Then, in New York, the East Coast center of the industry, he'd overseen the opening of a recording and video studio with state-of-the-art equipment—Sony Studios, exclusively for Sony artists—to be able to keep the whole process in-house, and therefore reduce the costs of using outside studios (and which soon became the home of "MTV Unplugged").

What all this showed was that Tommy Mottola, apart from being an astute businessman, was precisely the creative figure that Mariah had made him out to be. He had vision, and he was definitely looking to the future. Such are the requirements of the nineties executive. Being good, even very good, was no longer enough. The music industry, like every other, has become like a chess game, and to succeed, it is vital to think several moves ahead, anticipating what your rivals might do, and to be prepared to counter it while at the same time putting yourself in an advantageous position.

This was what Tommy had achieved. Sony was strong now, not just in record sales, but in many areas of the business. So he had fully earned the promotion from president of Sony Music (U.S.) to president/COO (Chief Operating Officer) of Sony Music. This moved him from a purely domestic to a global market. He would become responsible for more than sixty markets and eleven thousand employees—which would continue to include America. He would, he announced, continue the policies he'd implemented, of long-term artist development and aggressive management and marketing. What had worked in the United States should, after all, work elsewhere.

This new position rounded off a very good year for Mottola. He'd married a woman who was probably the hottest singing talent in the country, and then he'd been named to a new job. What else could happen to make it better?

Well, there was one thing. His new wife could have another hit album. Not only would he be able to be proud of her, but the bottom line on the company's balance sheet would look a whole lot better.

7

D reamlover" was the first release from Mariah's forth-coming album, *Music Box,* her first release in over a year. Doubtless the marketing department at Columbia was a little worried; "I'll Be There" had made number 1, but that was an oldie, a song that had been around for more than twenty years, familiar to many people. Of the material released from *Emotions,* only the title track had reached the top of the charts. Even if the other releases had all managed to make the Top Five, it still didn't have quite the same cachet. On top of that, neither *Emotions* nor *MTV Unplugged* had managed to hit the top album spot. That the record-buying public would be happy to hear and purchase Mariah's new songs wasn't the question; the question was just *how* happy would they be? And as if that wasn't enough pressure, the artist the label was now handling had just become the boss's wife! It would be in everyone's best interests if things went very smoothly.

The way things went, they needn't have worried unduly. In the middle of August the single glided into the charts at number 13, rising over the next couple of weeks to number 9, then number 3, before hitting the magical number 1 on the *Billboard* Hot 100 on September 4, 1993, Labor Day weekend. The only real surprise, and a very joyous one, was that it hogged that spot for a total of eight weeks, an absolute indication that, far from being on the wane, Mariah's popularity was still increasing.

As for the album itself, *Music Box* made its debut on the charts on September 17, and one week later stood poised at number 2, where it seemed to stall just shy of the top position, and indeed, it would be some time before it gained that elusive number 1 spot—until Christmas, to be exact, when its sales were undoubtedly boosted by copies purchased all over the country as gifts.

However, once it achieved number 1, *Music Box* was very reluctant to move down again. It stayed there for three weeks, slipped, then came back, slipped again and returned, until it ended up spending a total of eight weeks at the peak of the chart. And while that wasn't as impressive as *Mariah Carey*'s twenty-two weeks, it remained a very welcome statistic.

Even as "Dreamlover" began to fall through the Hot 100, the next single was being prepared for release. This was "Hero," a powerful, inspirational ballad, and it was destined for another swift rise, climbing to number 1 at the same time as the album did, on Christmas Day. This gave Mariah a remarkable total of eight number 1 *Billboard* singles, a feat bested by only nine artists in the entire history of the chart, and then only by such all-time greats as the Beatles (with twenty) and Elvis Presley (who had seventeen). Very few artists had managed more total weeks at number 1 than Mariah, either, who by this point had amassed twenty-eight. That she'd achieved all this before she was even twenty-four years old only made it more incredible, and showed that her future in music looked not merely rosy, but positively brilliant.

"Hero" would rapidly establish itself as a staple of MOR (middle of the road) radio, both AM and FM, to be enjoyed by all ages, as would its successor, Mariah's second-ever cover song—a sweeping, moving version of "Without You," which had been such a big, enduring hit for Harry Nilsson in the early seventies that it was generally assumed he'd written it. In actuality it had been penned by Pete Ham and Tommy Evans of the ill-fated British band Badfinger (both those songwriters would eventually commit suicide, troubled by financial problems), who had a number of hits themselves ("Come and Get It," "Day After Day," "No Matter What," "Baby Blue") which still receive frequent airplay on oldies stations.

But it was Nilsson's hit that Mariah had grown up with and loved, and which she used as the basis for her version. Mariah and Walter's arrangement owed a great deal to Nilsson's rendition, rather than to the original, although it did strip away some of the massive orchestration which tended to overwhelm the Nilsson cut.

In a rather sad, ironic footnote, on the day Mariah's version of "Without You" was released, Harry Nilsson, only in his early fifties, died from heart problems. However, the record was not withdrawn, but allowed to stand, at least in part as a tribute to his talent (he had released a number of excellent albums, and was a very talented songwriter in his own right). "Without You" entered the Hot 100 at the end of January 1994 at number 53, then climbed speedily, to numbers 35, 12, 7, then number 6 and number 4, where it remained for three weeks before managing one more small jump to number 3, where it stayed. That would be its peak.

Even though it never made number 1, "Without You" still enjoyed a long run on the charts, hovering in the Top Ten and never really falling until May, when the fourth single from *Music Box* was issued—another slow song, "Anytime You Need a Friend." This debuted at number 45, rising in its second week to number 32. It continued to climb until it stood at number 12 by the end of June.

Given the way Columbia had interspersed ballads and uptempo songs as singles for Mariah in the past, it might have seemed odd that for this album they'd mostly released slower material ("Dreamlover" stood as an exception, but even that was hardly a dance tune). After all, *Music Box* did contain two collaborations between Mariah, David Cole, and Robert Clivilles, just as *Emotions* had. The logic may have been, as stated earlier, that Mariah's real strength lay with ballads. Within that framework she could offer a very strong, emotional vocal, and let her voice, rather than the beat, dominate the song. "Hero" and "Without You" both offered excellent examples of this. Both used relatively simple vocal lines, but that simplicity was their real power. It was apparent from these songs that Mariah had learned a great deal about arranging a piece—as her partner, Walter Afanasieff, had learned about bringing out the best in her.

One of the first things to strike a listener of *Music Box* was the fact that Mariah barely touched her infamous upper register. This time around there was absolutely no reliance on that gimmick to sell her music, and in the brief instance it did occur, it provided a fitting climax to the material. Mariah was relying purely on her singing and her powers of interpretation to make the material work.

The other immediately noticeable factor was the production. As had been seen previously, Mariah was torn between two things—studio perfection and a raw, "live" sound. She loved to layer backing vocals, and her recordings utilized mostly synthesizers and drum machines—whereas live she utilized real instruments and a large number of backup singers. On *Music Box* it seemed as if she'd finally achieved a balance between the two apparently opposite ideals. She brought in a number of other people to sing behind her, and, although she continued to make full use of synthesizers (or, to be precise, Walter did), there was far more space in the overall sound, letting "some air" into the songs, as it were. Everything appeared much less produced than on *Emotions,* and most definitely much, much less produced than *Mariah Carey,* which seemed cluttered and overflowing by comparison.

As had been mentioned earlier, she'd also expanded her circle of writing collaborators, bringing in Dave Hall for one track ("Dreamlover"), and Babyface, a star in his own right, for another ("Never Forget You"). She continued to work very closely with Walter Afanasieff, with whom she cowrote six of the record's ten tracks, and Clivilles and Cole, who were drafted to help write, perform, and produce the two dance tunes. The overall effect of this was to offer some stylistic variety, both in the approach to the music, and the sound of the tracks.

This album also seemed to have less gospel and soul influence than its predecessors, which was a little surprising, given its overwhelming presence on *Unplugged*. Where it did occur, it tended to spring from the backing vocalists, who'd all sung with Mariah before, either on *Emotions* or on *MTV Unplugged*. About the only conclusion to be drawn was that Mariah was moving forward in her music, and that, however much she loved both those styles, it was time for her to progress and change a little. For, if *Emotions* had demonstrated her quick advancement from the material on *Mariah Carey,* then *Music Box* stood as a quantum leap forward.

She'd hinted at her growing sophistication all along, on songs like "Vanishing" and "The Wind," both of which made real use of her singing skill. But on this album she'd fully fused that ability into every song, not only in her own voice, but also in the vocal and instrumental arrangements. And while there was a danger that doing this might remove her somewhat from pop music into a more adult area (which was very likely the ultimate intention), the success of the singles would seem to show that she'd been able to retain her old audience, and that the public at large had embraced this "new" Mariah with wide-open arms. After all, "Hero" sold more than a million copies, "Without You" generated a gold disc, and *Music Box* itself went multi-platinum, with more than 6 million copies bought in the U.S. alone, and over a million more in the rest of the world; those were hardly the figures of an artist whose popularity was fading.

ASTONISHINGLY, the critics weren't happy with the album; they seemed to find it lacking in substance and emotion. In *Time* magazine, Christopher John Farley called it "perfunctory and almost passionless," although he did admit, "there are some great moments on *Music Box.* The gospel-flavored "Anytime You Need a Friend" demonstrates Carey's vocal power, although too fleetingly. And the title cut is one of Carey's loveliest songs to date. . . ." But then he felt, "One gets the sense that Carey is squandering her chance at greatness. . . ." In *Rolling Stone,* Stephen Holden agreed that her singing had undergone "some subtle but strategic stylistic shifts" in the wake of the *MTV Unplugged* EP, and he did find that Mariah's voice had "a sustained passion that enhances the record's wedding-album feel." In the end, though, his conclusion was that the album was "precisely calculated to be a blockbuster. . . ." Even *People* found praise only for "Dreamlover," "Without You," and "Anytime You Need a Friend," as reviewer Amy Linden declared that on the other tracks, "[t]he melodies lie limp and formless, waiting for the power of her fluid voice to give them shape."

It was, perhaps, to be expected. After the superlatives expended on the *MTV Unplugged* EP, Mariah was due for another critical backlash. It seems to stand somehow as a way of maintaining a balance of power, odd as that might sound, the reviewers' way of not letting the artists become too big and too popular. And while the critics may influence opinion to an extent, what really counts is the bottom line—how many people are willing to go and shell out those dollars they've earned for a record. In those terms, Mariah did indeed have a "blockbuster," although maybe not in quite the way the journalists had meant.

Making "Dreamlover" both the initial single and the album's leadoff track was a very sound choice. Although not typical of the album, it was a wonderful pop song, with a bouncy, breezy, summery feel—perfect for a tune released in the dog days of August. A mid-tempo song, ideal for foot-tapping, it was introduced by the hook line (which would be insistently repeated throughout), played on the synthesizer. The tune contained a sample of David Porter's "Blind Alley" (Porter is probably best known for his collaborations with soul singer Isaac Hayes in the sixties), well hidden in the melody, which swirled around Walter Afanasieff's warm Hammond organ sound. This was nothing less than high-quality pop music, which took its cues from neither soul nor gospel, but still maintained a "classic" feel over a nineties rhythm, and an atmosphere that was reminiscent of the Young Rascals' perfect summer hit of the sixties, "Groovin'." By itself, it offered all the evidence necessary to show Mariah's growth, as one of her very best and poppiest compositions to date. And if her lyrics, describing her "Dreamlover" and his qualities, were aimed at her husband . . . well, what could be wrong with that? Love can be a wonderful inspiration.

The video, directed by Diane Martel, picked up on the song's summery sheen with its images of Mariah swimming in a pool by a waterfall with her dog, Jack (she commented later that the water was so cold that she refused to swim until Martel dived in first), lying in a field of wildflowers, and singing in front of a group of hip-hop dancers. The casual feel, almost like clips from home movies edited together, captured the song's off-the-shoulder airiness, and its frequent appearances on the various video-music channels did nothing to hurt the song's success.

The next track also proved to be the next single, "Hero"—Mariah's most directly inspirational song yet, even more so than "Make It Happen." As she described it, "This song is saying you don't need someone to say, 'It's okay for you to do this.' If you look inside yourself, and you believe, you can be your own hero." A lush ballad which, from its popularity in a number of radio formats, may well go on to become a standard, it made impressive use of Mariah's lower alto register. Like so many of the pieces on the album, it was very emotional, building through the verses to the chorus where both the melody and the lyrics broke through—musically, from a sad, minor key to a happier, victorious major, and lyrically, with the joy of realizing that there is a power within, whatever name one might choose to give it.

"Anytime You Need a Friend" was another pop ballad where Mariah could let her voice roam free, and interestingly, when she did so, she again kept clear of her high register, preferring a low, rough growl. Once more there was a positive message in the words (as could be found in seven of the album's ten tracks). This song offered the only trace of gospel music on the record, and that was limited to the backing singers on the chorus; even then, it seemed muted, and more secular than holy. Had this been recorded for *Emotions* or *Mariah Carey*, it would probably have sounded very different—far smoother and more fully arranged, and most certainly with more of a gospel edge, although it worked splendidly in this context.

The album's title track continued the ballads. It had a subdued, sighing, contented tone, and such a gentle love song stood tall among Mariah's compositions. It required a great deal of control to sing properly, to keep the tune's softness and sweetness without resorting to volume, and at the same time to not go too far the other way and become saccharine. Mariah managed to maintain that delicate balance in a manner that seemed effortless, floating easily above Walter's keyboards and the shimmer of Michael Landau's guitars. Lyrically, with its promises of giving and commitment, it had the feel of wedding vows, and the tinkling music-box line played on the synthesizer conveyed the sense of a wedding cake with figures of the bride and groom perched on top.

After such a quiet piece came the record's first dance song, "Now That I Know," one of the two pieces Mariah cowrote and coproduced with the Clivilles-Cole team. After four mid- and slow-tempo songs, it offered a bright contrast, carried by the rhythm rather than the melody. Unfortunately, neither this nor "I've Been Thinking About You"—the other product of this joint effort which appeared on *Music Box*—was as strong as the dance tunes on *Emotions,* which may have been the ultimate reason neither song saw release as a single. To call them "filler" would be an exaggeration—Mariah has shown herself to be too much the perfectionist to allow such a thing—but neither is particularly memorable, a distinct disadvantage for a single. Again, the words are positive, of a person moving from uncertainty about a lover to being sure in her heart that love is real, which could be taken as a reflection of her own life.

While many reviewers have taken Mariah to task for her lyrics, generally dismissing them as trite and trivial, the truth is she has never been afraid to explore her emotions and open her heart in her songs. Never has that been more the case than on this record, where her joy is apparent throughout much of the album. Even the three sad pieces are full of compassion, however much it might be tempered by sorrow. While that might be expected from someone so deeply in love, it still remains a wonderful message to pass on, when so much that is released is either full of anger and hatred (rap) or apathy (a lot of grunge and alternative music). If it's the mainstream artists who accentuate the positive values like love and friendship, then all the better for them; at least, with their sales, they're striking a chord somewhere.

Those three sad pieces came together, beginning with "Never Forget You," Mariah's collaboration with Babyface, an R&B star with a number of hits to his credit. Another slow song, appropriately—since it lamented the loss of a love, albeit in a very tender way—it contained a lovely keyboard line that hovered over the verses. Mariah was able to indulge her passion for overdubbing her own voice for the backing vocals on the chorus. If any criticism could be leveled at the tune, it is that it slips by too quickly. In three-quarter, or waltz, time, it had an air of partners gliding around the dance floor in memories; indeed, the very fact that it wasn't in four-four, or straight, time made it stand out, and it could quite easily have been a hit single, with an appeal that would have easily transcended generational barriers.

As has been said, Mariah's version of "Without You" owed a great deal to Harry Nilsson's 1972 hit, which had stayed at number 1 on *Billboard*'s Hot 100 for four weeks. Over the years it had cropped up endlessly on oldies and MOR stations, to the point where it had virtually become a pop standard, with Nilsson's as the definitive version—which made

Mariah's decision to cover it a formidable proposition, since that would be what her interpretation would be measured against and judged by.

There was little cause for worry. Her execution was every bit as strong and tasteful as her work on "I'll Be There." From a simple piano opening, the verses remained quite stark, building to the grand swell of the chorus, where a powerful vocal was necessary to overcome the strong melody. Needless to say, that was no problem for Mariah, and the low harmony she used emphasized her lead line. The backing vocalists entered close to the end of the song, adding depth and grandeur, and allowing Mariah to play the diva—one of only two opportunities on the album—and to let her voice glide around the melody, once more in a low register.

Next to such a great song, "Just to Hold You Once Again" was almost bound to suffer in comparison, and in truth it wasn't Mariah's strongest writing effort. It was, however, somewhat redeemed by the use of the backing vocals, whose natural soulful tinge bolstered and added to the tune.

The song did play to Mariah's greatest strength, though— her ballad singing—and by *Music Box* that seemed beyond question to be where her real interest lay. Lyrically this is a despairing, confused tale, the singer still wondering *why* the breakup had to happen, even as the love refuses to leave her heart. It was only natural, with her increasing stature as an artist, that she would want to create something that might last, and with dance music becoming dated so quickly, ballads were the obvious choice.

"Just to Hold You Again" was followed by what stood as the album's most fascinating song, the other Carey-Clivilles-Cole collaboration, "I've Been Thinking About You" (coincidentally the title of a different song, a number 1 single in 1991 for the group Londonbeat). What made it so interesting were the production tricks employed throughout the first verse, where all the instruments except percussion were dropped from the mix behind Mariah's voice, to reappear very briefly at unusual intervals, an idea adapted from reggae/dub music. It certainly had the effect of catching the listener's attention and dragging it into the song.

As a song it probably stood as the most contemporary-sounding piece Mariah had committed to tape. While much of that was due to the production (and largely the rhythm track, at that), a great deal of the arrangement ideas came from modern R&B, which in turn had taken its cues from hip-hop. So everything ended up very jerky, with no real flow, or rather the flow seemed interrupted. It was pleasant enough, but after the depth of the ballads that preceded it, it sounded hollow, a shell without a center. One of the things that worked against it was its wordiness; merely fitting in the lines precluded the expression of emotion.

"All I've Ever Wanted" was the album's final track. Closing with a ballad was good, particularly one as strong as this. The song was vaguely reminiscent of Whitney Houston's gigantic international smash, "I Will Always Love You," but certainly not close enough for it to lose its own identity. And for an album that had dealt so much with love in such an honest and disarming way, this was an appropriate end, a simple love song quite obviously addressed to Tommy Mottola. That the melody was fairly basic was irrelevant; it was the words that were important here, echoing the sentiment of the title all the way through. It was a song that might in the future compete with Whitney's, to be sung at weddings, or at least at receptions.

The album as a whole had a great deal of power. It was a very personal statement, something the reviewers missed, and that may well have been the biggest piece of growth it demonstrated. Yes, musically it was more sophisticated, and often more subtle. But the words pushed it across the line into art. What the critics dismissed as "hackneyed high school poetry" really explored matters of faith—faith in love as a reason to carry on, and as an inspiration. "Mostly I'm choosing specifically to write lyrics that might inspire someone, because I've been blessed with a positive and incredible life," she said, adding, "I tell my stories in my own way."

That way connected very, very well. Ten months after its release *Music Box* still stood at number 16 on the *Billboard* album charts. It had been a top album in almost every country, from Japan to Europe to Australia. Four tracks had been released as singles, and all had been hits. It nearly equaled—and in some ways eclipsed—the success of her debut. Nowhere near as much publicity had surrounded its release, but it still sold virtually as many copies. *Mariah Carey,* even though it contained a number of ballads, was án exuberant album, full of youth and the joy of having gotten a recording contract. *Emotions* took that one step further. There was more complexity to the songs. The slow tunes cut deeper, the gospel and soul influences stood taller. *MTV Unplugged* was a side trip in Mariah's progress in some ways, a record that portrayed her live in an ideal situation. But, looking back from the perspective of *Music Box,* it could almost be viewed as the end of an era, the culmination of those soul and gospel influences.

Allowing plenty of space in which to write, arrange, and record, and to have time to relax and breathe in the process, *Music Box* stood as the first album of Mariah's full maturity. At twenty-three, she'd already been involved in the music business for seven years, and had seen a great deal of bad before the good arrived. She was older than her years, and that was bound to come across in her music. As she said in an interview, "I've been disillusioned a lot. . . . I think I'm constantly being let down. I'm sure I'm a giving person and a loyal person. I've tried to hold on to friends from high school, but suddenly it's 'Oh, I know her.' I'm like a topic of conversation. Since I was a kid I've always thought of myself as a hard-ass, always smart, streetwise, not vulnerable—but I am."

She'd also realized the power in what she did: "One person could say 'Hero' is a schmaltzy piece of garbage, but another person can write me a letter and say, 'I've considered committing suicide every day of my life for the last ten years until I heard that song and I realized after all I can be my own hero.' And that, that's an unexplainable feeling, like I've done something with my life, y'know? . . . it meant something to someone." And with that realization the coyness which had sometimes marked her early work vanished. She was beginning to produce the work she was capable of; she had, in other words, "grown into" her art. That was also apparent in her singing on *Music Box.* By staying in her lower register almost the whole time, she focused attention on its power and emotive ability (not to mention on the song), rather than all the octave tricks she could have managed. Someone with less confidence would have made more use of her gimmicks.

So this was a turning point, the start of a new musical chapter for Mariah. She'd taken stock, and she seemed to be pointing herself in a new direction. The up-tempo dance songs appeared to be there more because they were expected than anything; her heart didn't seem to be in them. But even Barbra Streisand had made a concession to the times once, in the seventies, and released a disco album. For Mariah to have released an album composed entirely of ballads, even with a mid-paced tune like "Dreamlover," might have alienated a younger audience. For the moment she was still hedging her bets. And who was to say she was wrong? From the sales, she'd apparently struck exactly the right note. As they say, you can't argue with success, and Mariah had certainly had plenty of that.

8

Before *Music Box* even hit the streets, Mariah's first tour had been planned. In 1992 she had said to Stephen Holden in the *New York Times*, "I'm not into performing. . . . If I toured, I wouldn't have had another album out for at least another year. It's so hard on my voice. . . . When I go out there people don't want to hear me just breeze through them [the songs]. They want to hear every note."

So the announcement of the venture came as something of a surprise, albeit a very pleasant and welcome one. What had changed her mind? It was never revealed, but it might well have been the enthusiastic reception her "MTV Unplugged" performance received. For someone who had claimed such shyness, and who said she felt uneasy on stage, she'd appeared completely at home there. It might have been a controlled studio environment, but she still had to interact with and relate to the audience—a job she'd done like a pro.

It wasn't going to be an extensive tour. Quite the opposite, really. A total of just five dates, four on the East Coast, with another outside Chicago. But the fact that it was happening at all was enough to excite fans and to ensure that they'd be waiting in line when the tickets went on sale.

In many ways the shows could be viewed as a way of testing the waters. Spread over a little more than a month, they offered a schedule which didn't put any strain on Mariah's voice with exhaustive traveling or staying in hotels. More importantly, they allowed her (and her management) to gauge just how extensive the demand was to see her live, in a way that could leave open the possibility of a longer tour at some later date. Or, perhaps, to offer a series of nights at selected venues around the country.

The concerts were set to happen in November and December of 1993, beginning in Miami, Florida. But well before that, the rehearsals had begun and negotiations successfully completed for a performance that would expose Mariah to millions, and without any of them having to leave the comfort of their homes.

Her star status, and the overwhelming acceptance of her MTV show had been enough to inspire someone to suggest a special on television. There was certainly plenty of precedent for it. Barbra Streisand had done several such shows in the sixties, all of which did astonishingly well in the ratings. NBC picked up on the idea, contracts were exchanged, and the wheels set in motion.

While some might have wondered what form it would take—would it be a variety program, with Mariah singing a few songs, then introducing guests? or perhaps there'd be some sort of theme?—the obvious idea was a Mariah Carey concert. Wonderful as "Unplugged" had been, it wasn't a *real* performance, in a theater. Such a format would serve two purposes: It would bring Mariah's live show to many, many people who wanted to see her but who lived too far from the cities where she'd be playing on tour, and the filming would serve as a warm-up for the tour itself.

By now Mariah had surrounded herself with a core group of top-notch musicians and singers. Most of them had worked with her on the last two studio albums and on the MTV appearance. They'd become used to her, and were all full of admiration, not just for her singing ability and technique, but also for her utterly professional attitude toward every aspect of her music.

Having such people undoubtedly made the grinding procedure of rehearsals easier. They would also add an extra dimension to her show—in place of the studio synthesizers and computers. Live, it would have to be *real* instruments, with real sparks created between human performers, just like "Unplugged" but on a more elaborate scale.

There was never any doubt that Walter Afanasieff would be the musical producer of the show. He and Mariah had worked so closely for three years that they'd become almost like brother and sister. And Mariah trusted him completely. Probably only Tommy Mottola knew her better. Essentially the lineup that began rehearsals was the same one which had backed her on MTV. Walter played piano and Hammond organ, and directed the musicians. Vernon Black was on guitar, Randy Jackson on bass, Gigi Conaway on drums; Dan Shea played keyboards. About the only changes were that Ren Klyce was now also playing keyboards, instead of percussion, and Peter Michael had replaced Sammy Figueroa as percussionist. The singers had all worked with her before, too: Cindy Mizelle (her old friend from the days when Mariah was scuffling for session work), Deborah Cooper, Melanie Daniels, and Kelly and Shanrae Price.

Strings would be added for some of the numbers, with a base of five players who would be augmented by the Empire State Youth Orchestra. But they were extra, the icing on the television cake. The others were the ones who'd be taking the show on the road.

The program's director would be another face familiar to Mariah—Larry Jordan, or Lawrence, as he was now called. After working with her on "Unplugged" and on some of her videos, he knew full well what to look for and expect from her.

It was interesting that NBC chose to air Mariah's special on Thanksgiving, for it could only have meant that they anticipated very strong ratings for the show. The holiday is traditionally a time for families to be together, so programs with the highest ratings tend to be those which appeal to more than one sex or age group. In other words, they were banking on her being counted as vital viewing by not only the kids, but also moms and dads and grandparents—a sure sign that Mariah had gone beyond being a mere pop singer and was on her way to becoming a true entertainer.

The show was to be filmed at Proctor's Theatre, located in

Schenectady, New York, an easy commute from Mariah's up-state home. An ornate, venerable building, it turned out to be an excellent location for both the set and the cameras, with a stage big enough to accommodate all the participants without seeming overcrowded. The video of the concert, released in time for Christmas, captured the event in all its glory, including extra footage of interviews with the band, Mariah and her mother, and the wrap party for the program (as well as the "Dreamlover" video).

The theater was packed with fans, mostly in their teens and early twenties. Some had banners saying WE LOVE YOU or YOU'RE THE BEST, MARIAH. The area directly in front of the stage was crowded with those just wanting to be close and maybe touch their hero.

From the audience's viewpoint, the band took up the left side of the stage, and to the right stood the singers, with the string players behind them. The set, of a cityscape, was simple but powerful, with plenty of lights, shining both onto the stage and into the auditorium, to create effects that would, at times, appear almost surreal.

Mariah's entrance was greeted with a standing ovation, a very generous gesture for her first major public show. She was dressed in her trademark black (as were all the other participants, which had also been the case for the "MTV Unplugged" performance), in a long, flowing dress which was slit up both sides. Around her neck she wore the heart-shaped pendant which had made its debut in the "Love Takes Time" video, and on her left hand the huge diamond of her wedding ring caught the light.

She opened with a favorite, "Emotions," appearing relaxed and even glad to be there. The musicians swung with the beat, and the kick of a real band seemed to put an edge on her singing. Not quite as raw as her MTV show, it was still less polished than her records, allowing her the freedom to weave around the lines more, and to interplay with the backup vocalists, with whom she frequently traded smiles. The sound, it should be noted, was superb, everything as clear as a studio recording.

After the rapturous reception the song drew, she lowered the energy level by singing "Hero." Cameras panning across the audience showed many singing along, taking in the full meaning of the lyrics, which came across far more strongly here than on *Music Box,* sung with the emotion of the moment. Whatever accusations had been leveled at Mariah, being a plastic performer, just mouthing the words, hadn't been among them, and here she seemed to consider every line before it came out of her mouth, and delivered it forcefully.

Notably, even live she used her upper register very sparingly, relying, as on *Music Box,* on the quality of her voice rather than any trickery to push her songs across.

"Hero" was followed by a costume change, into wide flared black pants, a shiny black T-shirt, and a thin quilted vest. The new clothes brought another tempo change, accelerating the pace again with "Someday," Mariah's third number 1. The band showed their true worth here, able to inject some funk under the melody and truly kick it along, projecting the feel of a steamy dance club into Proctor's Theatre as the crowd swayed and sang along in time, while Mariah prowled from side to side like a lioness, her hair becoming more attractively tousled as she moved. She brought out two of the singers into the spotlight with her, trading voices on the choruses, a very impressive display of vocal power on the part of all three, letting it build as the instruments dropped out, until the song reached its triumphant climax.

After this came another ballad, "Without You," from the newest album (this footage would be the song's video). It was an understated version, gathering all the more strength because of it, and a firm reminder of why Mariah has so often described her music as "vocally driven." She and the backing singers worked so well together that the instrumental accompaniment was virtually unnecessary, the swell of the chorus rising mightily. Even so, as on the recorded version, there was very little gospel feel to it, but rather an emphasis of the lyrics' huge sense of loss.

For "Make It Happen," Mariah began the song sitting on the edge of the stage, as hands pressed toward her and faces looked up and sang along on her most autobiographical song. Even with such close personal contact she seemed quite comfortable, as if the audience's warmth was giving her a boost. But by the first chorus she was on her feet and moving around the stage, and things began to really loosen up.

"Dreamlover" brought the show's only color to the stage, in the form of three coordinated hip-hop dancers with bright T-shirts. By this time the strings had been cleared away, with their chairs and music stands, leaving plenty of space. The dancers' presence at the rear of the stage, ignored by everyone else, seemed a little out of place. By her own admission, Mariah is no dancer, and no one probably expected to see her moving with them (unlike, say, Madonna), but the way they were used came across almost as an afterthought, a late concession to the youthful audience. Which was a shame, because they were good (interestingly, the choreography was by Diane Martel, who had also directed the "Dreamlover" video; obviously a woman of many talents), although they might have been better used on a faster tune, like "Someday." Still, it was more the fact that the camera concentrated on them, rather than the dancing itself, which made them seem intrusive. And had there been some interaction between them and Mariah, however small, then they would have seemed to fit in.

But the song worked, still as bubbling and friendly as a summer's day, one of the best pop tunes of the nineties and quite justifiably Mariah's biggest hit, and it transformed the auditorium into a grassy meadow on an August afternoon, as people all over the theater began to smile at the song's opening notes.

The spotlights dramatically caught her at the rear of the stage after the opening chords of "Love Takes Time," and *dramatic* was the ideal adjective to describe her reading of the song, full of wrenching emotion, truly giving it everything she's got. If her version of the tune on "Unplugged" had seemed low-key, this was quite the opposite. Indeed, for the rest of the show Mariah seemed to slip into a higher gear emotionally to put her material across, and to finish on a metaphoric (if not literal) high note.

Musically this was identical to the recorded version; what gave the song its kick was her performance. Contrasting this (and, later, "Vision of Love") with the original hit, Mariah's growth over three years became quite apparent. The younger Mariah had belted the songs out, it seemed. They attacked you. The more mature woman, even with more emotion, sang with far more subtlety. She still retained the excitement, but had tempered it with experience and control, a guaranteed winning combination.

Another costume change brought Mariah back for the show's final segment. She reappeared in a long, tight, sleeveless black dress with a high neck, slit on the side to make movement easier.

"Anytime You Need a Friend," the fourth song performed from *Music Box,* was arranged to pay homage to Mariah's love of gospel music with the use of the Refreshing Springs Church Choir, taking up the center stage behind Mariah, who perched on a stool. In their white robes the choir offset the other performers, and with the other five backup singers formed a huge wall of vocal sound, which was used to good effect here. At the same time, though, it's impossible to wonder whether their presence wouldn't have been better served by a song that was overtly gospelish, such as "If It's Over." However, Mariah was still able to wail over the assembled voices, and proved that, although the music she performed was changing, her heart remained in the same place, and probably always would.

"Vision of Love," the slinky song which had introduced Mariah to the world, was greeted passionately by the crowd, who seemed intent on weighing her down with bouquets of roses, offerings she gathered from their hands as she sang.

There was a cocky edge to the performance; it wasn't dismissive of the tune—quite the opposite, more like treating it as an old friend who didn't need to be handled gently. As a climax to the show it was perfect. It had been around long enough to have been heard—and recognized—by a great many people. The lyrics focused on positive sentiments, looking ahead, and its tempo was a little faster than much of the material Mariah had performed during the evening. But, more than anything, it left everyone wanting more, the very best thing anyone on-stage can ask for.

That wasn't the last song, though. That spot was reserved for an intimate rendition of "I'll Be There," performed on the theater's stage for a group of inner-city children sponsored by New York City's Police Athletic League, a charity with which Mariah had become actively involved. Mariah and the other performers were all casually dressed, and the moment captured a version of the tune that, while obviously well rehearsed, still had the spark of spontaneity. Even Trey Lorenz was on hand to sing the part he'd made justifiably famous, and Mariah's voice was an eerie imitation of a young Michael Jackson, to the point where one could close one's eyes and not be certain of the difference. The kids, of course, loved it, gazing in frank adoration at Mariah, oblivious to the cameras trained on them, filming their reactions. It was a special moment, and one well worth keeping. The softness of the song let the viewer down gently, giving an appropriate end to the show.

What cannot be overstated is the importance of this program. It had been something of a test for Mariah, one she passed with honors as a stage performer. The filming had to have been grueling. What made it onto the screen was only a part of a long, tedious process. For every change that seemed to happen like magic, there was a great deal of work, including the laborious setting up and tearing down of microphones and chairs. In reality Mariah did not just vanish into the wings to return a moment later in a new dress, looking fresh and glamorous. And in some ways that made heroes of the audience, for having the stamina to wait it all out to be able to see their idol, and it also shows just how dedicated her fans could be.

Above all, Mariah had managed to make it an occasion. Pop concerts are a dime a dozen. You can find them in any major city almost every night of the week. But to make one stand out requires something special. A performer who's rarely seen live is a good start; a performer who can really cut it live, and offer the audience some entertainment, something that goes well beyond simple, mechanical versions of the hits, is what being a star is all about.

And, quite noticeably, Mariah was relatively adventurous in her choice of material for the evening. It would have been very easy for her to have performed all her hits. As it was, she didn't even perform all her number 1 songs, leaving out the powerful "I Don't Wanna Cry." Four of the tunes came from *Music Box,* and while the album had been a big seller for almost three months, a large proportion of the viewing audience couldn't have been familiar with it except for the hit single. Four out of a total of ten songs is a pretty large percentage, and showed that Mariah wasn't just someone happy to sit on her laurels, but was willing to take chances.

As might have been predicted, given the direction Mariah's music was taking, there was a large concentration on ballads, a further indication that this would almost certainly be the way of the future for her.

IT MIGHT WELL HAVE BEEN HOPED that this show would help make her a star of the same magnitude as, say, Barbra Streisand, a face that would be immediately recognizable by the American public. If that was the intent, then this hadn't been a success. While it painted Mariah's talents very clearly, she didn't show Streisand's breadth or scope. But the fact that someone who such a brief time before hadn't looked forward to being in front of an audience, could come across as so pleasant and natural—almost the classic girl next door—augured well for the future. She was the "nice" girl, as opposed to Madonna's engineered nastiness, and niceness is a quality with far more longevity and acceptance in the public mind. So, something was certainly achieved that night. She'd established her niche in the general consciousness as something more than another pop singer. The people who'd just heard her in passing on the radio could now put a face (and a smile) to the voice. And that made it a big deal.

"I was okay until I had to walk up this ramp onto the stage and I heard this deafening scream and it was kinda like everything in my life, this whole incredible whirlwind I'd been going through, it had all been leading up to that insane moment—and there I was."

MIAMI ARENA is a huge concrete hall, not exactly the best place to hear music of any kind. The size and construction of the building obliterates any kind of subtlety. For the first night of a tour it was almost like an enemy, designed to undermine the sound in squalls of feedback and thumping bass notes. For Mariah, it had to be something of an ordeal, a trial by fire.

The filming of the special had been fine, but this, now, was what live performance was all about: factors out of the artist's control, music that bounced back from the far wall. And, to make it worse, not all 16,000 seats had been sold. That many people would have had a dampening effect and there would have been less reverberation. As it was, only some 10,000 people turned out, mostly young couples who had brought their children along. ". . . The audience—they knew it was my first show, they were very supportive." But Mariah was nervous. That was quite obvious from the reviews, one of which said, "Carey seemed to shrink during between-song patter. Opening-night jitters led her to repeat 'Thank you' and 'I'm so happy to be here' more often than seemed natural." Still, that's hardly surprising when confronted with a concrete monstrosity that attempts to stop you from hearing yourself.

It was a big show she took on the road, more or less the same as had been seen on television, including the full gospel choir. For someone who was still widely perceived as a young pop star, that made it a risky venture. On TV, editing cuts out the time between songs, the exits for costume changes, and so on, but in the flesh they can ruin the pace of a show.

The stage set was elaborate, described by Sandra Schulman in *Billboard* as looking "oddly like an industrial church." But it was used largely as a backdrop, despite the platforms which were there. The main effect was the lighting, pinpointing the performers and also shining and sweeping into the crowd.

Needless to say, the band and backing singers were all in black, as was Mariah herself, even through all the costume changes, which had her in a leather jacket, a bodysuit, and even a gorgeous gown with a glittering necklace that she put on for the encore. As on the special, what color came onto the stage was courtesy of the choir and the dancers.

Singing, she appeared quite at ease, grinning, relishing each song, and in excellent, strong voice. The times she did utilize that upper register brought the audience to its feet, cheering—the vocal gymnastics were evidently one of the things they'd come for.

Although she was only playing to two-thirds a capacity crowd, Mariah still gave the show everything she had. On-stage for an hour and fifteen minutes, she sang all her hits (they were, after all, her drawing card), including "I'll Be There," and added another cover song, a soul hit from the mid-eighties by the SOS Band, "Just Be Good to Me" (which, interestingly, had been revived three years before by Beats International in a reggae version, "Dub Be Good to Me," an international hit). She moved around the stage as if she owned it—and, for seventy-five minutes, she did. Especially notable were her renditions of "Make It Happen" and "Vision of Love," where the interplay between the performers ignited and soared to create something magical, much more than the sum of its parts.

The crowd loved it, as they were meant to and as they should have. In a time when encores seem a mandatory part of any show, scripted into the set list, Mariah's was earned, and the clapping and whistling made the requests for "More" utterly genuine, particularly coming from such a sedate group.

By most standards the night could have been termed a success, especially for a singer's first real outing. The people who'd paid to see her went home happy. But with the show over, it was the critics' turn to have their say. "Well, there were a lot of critics out to get me," Mariah said later, when the tour was well behind her. " 'This girl's sold all these albums, she's never toured, let's get her.' So they did. I turned on the TV in bed that night and the CNN guy was saying, 'The reviews are in and it's bad news for Mariah Carey.' It really hurt me a lot." The backlash had hit once again.

Happily, though, although she was angry, she was still able to sort out what she saw as "valid criticism" and took that to heart, using it to make the rest of the tour better.

Billboard looked at the Miami show quite fairly. The magazine found much to praise and very little to fault, certainly in Mariah's performance. The reviewer's only advice was that ". . . this concert seemed to be a bit too much too soon. A smaller venue with a more intimate setting would have shown off Carey's presence and ability to better advantage." Not unkind words at all.

THE NEXT SHOW—a week later, on November 9 at The Centrum in Worcester, Massachusetts, near Boston—showed that she'd listened, and had fine-tuned her performance. A sellout crowd of 11,046 watched her weave magic out of thin air—all managed, she said, because "I took all the anger and put it out there in my next show." It certainly helped that it was one of those perfect nights musicians occasionally have, where everything clicks, and it's impossible to do any wrong. After the opening act—up-and-coming folk duo The Story had warmed up the audience—Mariah appeared beaming, striding across the stage, truly singing her heart out in front of a band that didn't just get behind the beat, they kicked it along. Whatever jitters she'd felt in Miami had been exorcised; if she'd seemed in good voice there, in New England she'd never sung better. The material was the same as the last show, but seemed fresh, as if this was a hungry young group, still scratching around and looking for its big break, rather than seasoned, precise professionals.

The audience was with her from the first note—before that, even. And as the evening progressed and they were caught up in her spell, it was impossible for them not to know something remarkable was going on while they watched. She didn't have to win them over, they were already hers, but she did it anyway, taking the time to chat with them between numbers, coming across as personable, relaxed, and confident.

It was certainly enough to make a believer out of the *Boston Globe*'s critic, who admitted he'd been a skeptic before the show. The review he turned in was nothing short of an unqualified rave, praising ". . . a spectacular performance . . . [which] bowled over the crowd with a confidence that grew before their very eyes." If Mariah had harbored any doubts in her mind about her ability to put on a live show that did justice to her talents (and, after the comments in Miami, she might have had some), those words would have convinced her that she could do it. The tour, which she'd agreed to, in part, "to give something back to the fans," was giving them an unexpected bonus—a glimpse of Mariah Carey starting to become the next Barbra Streisand.

If one moment can ever be seen as a turning point, that night at The Centrum was it for Mariah. She moved to a new level with her performance, and achieved something even she might not have been aware she was capable of doing. And with it came the realization that she could do it again, and that she would *want* to recapture that incredible feeling. It was a new goal to strive for—no bad thing, since she'd already managed to achieve all her others. And it most definitely permanently closed the door on any talk that she was simply a studio artist or any kind of manufactured star. She could stand very well on her own two feet, thank you.

And she knew how she'd managed it. "[I] let go all my inhibitions and just lost myself in performing." The rest—the applause, the praise—all flowed out of that.

It's a testament to her that she was able to maintain the level of intensity for the remaining tour dates. Granted, there were only three of them, but magic is a difficult thing to conjure out of the blue. It probably helped that there was time between them for her to regroup (performing on a high level night after night when you also have to find time to sleep, eat, and travel is virtually a superhuman task), and that the final show, at New York's Madison Square Garden, was more or less a homecoming for the Long Island girl. Nonetheless, it was something that went beyond the usual level of professionalism. Someone paying upward of $22.50 (the cheapest ticket price on the tour—the highest was $37.50) has a right to see a professional performance. What most of the thousands who came out to see Mariah saw was something far greater.

After Worcester, there was an eight-day break before a show on November 17 at the Rosemont Horizon, in Rosemont, Illinois, outside Chicago. Once more, it was a sellout, with 9,438 fans crammed into the theater. The time gap between gigs allowed the stage set to be hauled from New England to the Midwest and erected. It also allowed the performers a chance to go home to their families, rest, and recharge their batteries—most particularly Mariah, who, much as she enjoyed traveling, had no love of hotels, where it was difficult to sleep, and their canned air, which affected her throat. And she was almost certainly still enough of a newlywed to not want to be away from her husband a moment longer than necessary.

The group Theory opened the show, but it was Mariah people were waiting to see. Naturally, as she took the stage, there was a gigantic eruption of applause and cheers. It had already become the norm, but such a welcome was still an enormous rush for Mariah. It told her that the audience was with her every step of the way, rooting for her.

The set list—the songs to be performed—duplicated all the previous shows. Once again Mariah managed to find that kick of energy, that spark to ignite the evening and make it into something very memorable for those in attendance. None of the practicalities had changed since Miami. There were still the costume changes, the gospel choir, the dancers. But New England had affected a change on everyone. The music had an edge. The dance tunes bounced more and got the audience moving. The ballads had a sad, desperate edge. And yet again the critics were convinced that Mariah was more than a pop-chart confection.

THEN THERE WAS A two-week break over Thanksgiving. Of course, during that time Mariah's TV special was aired on NBC, giving her a larger crowd than any audience she could draw into a theater. When the crew returned to the road, it was for a short journey from New York to Philadelphia, and a date on the second of December.

Without any doubt, there was a warm atmosphere to this show, for Mariah's good friend and protégé, Trey Lorenz, was the opening act. His album had done well, as had the single from it—more than enough to be very encouraging for the future—and this date would show that he too was a force to be considered as a live performer.

The show was a sellout. Over twelve thousand people filled the Spectrum to see Mariah. For many of them, Trey's set was a bonus, music that was like Mariah's, a sweet singer with a gentle personality. It was all very nice, but it wasn't Mariah. And, polite as they were, they'd paid $25 and up to see the real thing.

Which they did. And once more Mariah charmed them

with her naturalness, amazed them with her voice and her songs, and kept the real world at bay for a while. She created a cocoon, a little world for everybody in the hall, a spun shell of notes. Magic.

THE FINAL, FIFTH SHOW came eight days later, on December 10. At New York's Madison Square Garden, it was, as mentioned, a hometown show. After all, Mariah was a born-and-raised New Yorker: she knew these people, if not individually, then by attitude, by history. She could relate to them all quite easily.

But there was also a downside to being a homegirl. She would be looked at more closely. The reviewers would be sharpening their knives. And everyone would expect *more* from her, special treatment. Not only was it hometown, it was *New York*, where every performer is supposed to give something extra. And it was the last date of the tour.

It was by far the biggest concert of her career. Philadelphia had brought out twelve thousand, quite a crowd, but the Garden holds 15,627. There are plenty of towns in the country that are smaller than that.

As it turned out, Mariah didn't quite manage to sell out the place. Taking up 96 percent of the building's capacity, 15,050 people paid from $28.50 to $37.50 to spend the evening with her—still very respectable, when long-established acts often sell far fewer tickets.

So Mariah went into the show with something to prove. She'd managed to wow them elsewhere, now it was the Big Apple's turn. If the reviewers carped because she was playing arenas and stadiums on her first tour, well, she'd show them why.

What she gave them was what she'd given Miami, Boston, Chicago, and Philly—herself, every little bit, singing her heart out—enough to impress Jon Pareles in the *New York Times*, who noted, "Beyond any doubt, Ms. Carey's voice is no studio

concoction. . . . [R]ock concerts aren't known for precise into-
nation, she sang with startling exact pitch." His description of
the show as "triumphant" was a high accolade from such a
respected newspaper, which isn't prone to giving this type of
praise lightly.

There was no reason to change anything from the previous
shows, but Mariah did make one alteration. For the encore she
reappeared, not in her customary black, but wearing a festive
red gown which reflected splendidly in the stage lights, to sing
a Christmas song, a reminder of the season and a playful way
to bring things to a close.

For "Just Be Good to Me" Mariah wore a black leather cap
of the type associated with seventies discos. When the song
ended, she took it from her head and tried to fling it into the
audience. Unfortunately, it somehow ended up behind her,
which amused not only the crowd, but cracked up everyone
onstage—including Mariah. She picked it up, commented on
how weak a future she had in professional sports, and tried
again. This time she succeeded, and the people loved it. It
made her one of them, human and fallible; the only difference
was that she'd made it, and it made them realize that they
could, too.

On a more sober note, the concert came a week after the
incident on the Long Island Rail Road where a gunman killed
several commuters and wounded a number of others. Introducing "Hero," Mariah announced that the profits from the
single would be donated to a fund which had been started to
aid the families of the victims. It was a remarkably generous
gesture (especially since the single would go on to become
number 1), a Long Islander doing something to help her neigh-
bors, and all the better for not being widely trumpeted in the
press. To tell this crowd was right—the event had hit close to
home and shaken them—and appropriate.

* * *

AND SO THE TOUR ENDED. Her "flamboyance was just right" for large stages. She proved to the world at large that she could be a very strong live performer. While the tour might not have satisfied everyone—there were still too many parts of the country she hadn't played—they at least had the consolation of the television special. Mariah's career had advanced by stages, and she'd conquered another one. The question was, what next?

9

It should come as no surprise that Mariah Carey in 1995 is somewhat different from the girl who left home to seek fame and fortune in 1987. She has said that she hasn't changed, and there is much that remains the same, most obviously her good, true heart. But her life has taken quite a number of turns she never could have predicted back then. In many ways, she's become two people—Mariah Carey the star, and Mrs. Tommy Mottola, wife of a very powerful record executive. Naturally, the two roles come together very often, but there's also a separation.

As a career woman, she has plenty going on. "Dreamlover" was nominated for a Grammy, but surprisingly, it didn't win, although its obvious popularity (as a single it sold more than a million copies) helped make up for the loss. *Music Box,* oddly, wasn't even nominated. However, it looks set to go on to become Mariah's best-selling record to date. And it leaves Mariah with a large number of options. There seems to be much less emphasis on the dance material, which was, to an extent, pushed on both *Mariah Carey* and *Emotions* to the point that both "Someday" and "Emotions" were remixed and released in extended versions. Neither of the dance songs on *Music Box* has seen release as a single. So it seems likely, as said before, that there will be more of a concentration on ballads, which will allow her to cross over to wider markets, and bring in older listeners. The long-term plan may well be to make her into a Streisand-type entertainer, the type who plays occasional concerts and performs for several nights at a time in Las Vegas or Atlantic City (which doesn't necessarily mean she'll become a Wayne Newton type of performer!).

Early in her career, after the success of the first album, Mariah professed that she had no interest in movies, or acting of any kind. She was, and intends to remain, committed solely to music. Will that change? It could. Time has shown that she's exceedingly photogenic, and her name on any theater marquee would guarantee an audience. In all likelihood she's already had offers; Hollywood is always quick to jump on any possibilities to increase its revenue. However, Madonna tried that route, in an effort to widen her scope, and to say it didn't pay off would be to put things kindly. Of course, the fact that she appeared in a number of films that all the critics hated didn't help matters, but the overall effect on her career was quite detrimental. Mariah is not Madonna, obviously, but there can be no doubt that she (and Tommy) looked and learned from the Blonde One's errors. Granted, Whitney Houston made a splash in *The Bodyguard,* but there was precious little praise for her acting skill. So, in the final analysis, given Mariah's acknowledged quest for perfection in everything she undertakes, the chances of her appearing on the big screen in the foreseeable future are probably quite slim.

Music is her priority, pure and simple. Whether it's as a singer, a writer, or a producer, it's what she does. She'll certainly continue to record, but not at the rate she began. There was more of a gap between the *MTV Unplugged* EP and *Music Box* than there had been between her other releases, and that will probably widen even more. The need to prove herself is gone; she's already shown she can do it all. So it will probably be that she'll adopt the industry standard of some two years between albums. That will mean that—since she's continually writing—she'll have a large number of completed songs to choose from for her albums, which will translate into an even higher quality of record. Combine that with her ongoing growth (and make no mistake, it will definitely continue) and increase in skill, Mariah will become a formidable proposition as a songwriter as time goes by. It would come as no surprise to find a number of other performers beginning to record some of her material.

As a producer she probably pretty much has a free hand to record whomever she might choose. Her name alone carries a lot of weight, and, vocally, almost a guarantee of quality (just look at Trey Lorenz, for example). And she has expressed the desire to undertake more production work, possibly with a contemporary gospel act, although it's a strong bet that she'll do a hands-on job, including a lot of her own backing vocals. She has an ear for a good song (her own records have shown that all too well), and no one would doubt her ability to recognize a good singer.

But while songwriting for others and producing are things she's explored with Trey, she has yet to follow up on them. In all fairness, her life has been so busy that she hasn't really had the time. But these days she's not in quite as much of a rush, so both might become larger factors in her life.

However, her focus is always likely to be her own singing, and her own albums. From her activities so far she will likely remain a recording artist much more than a live performer. Any tours she does undertake in the future will probably resemble her 1993 foray, a few selected dates with gaps of at least a week between shows. But, sooner or later, she will have to play in the South, the West, overseas, all the areas where audiences are eager to see her. It'll take a few years yet before she reaches Streisand's status of being able to perform a run of shows in New York and have them all sell out in an hour, with people traveling all over the country to see her. But it could well happen. Maria is close to thirty years younger than Barbra; she has time on her side.

And while she might still be generally regarded as a pop singer, that is changing. The NBC special of Thanksgiving 1993 had a great deal to do with that—for image is largely perception, and that television show changed the way people perceived her. She started to become an entertainer. And that seems to be the future.

It appeared, as 1994 progressed, that Mariah might finally take some time for herself. "Anytime You Need a Friend" peaked at number 12, and no further singles from the album appeared. Summer became fall, and "Music Box" remained in the Top 100 of the *Billboard* album charts.

However, Mariah wasn't destined to stay away from the singles chart too long. She returned, accompanying Luther Vandross in a duet, a remake of the song "Endless Love," which had been such a huge hit for Diana Ross and Lionel Richie in 1981, when it sold more than 2 million copies. This version, which was taken from Luther's album, was produced by Walter Afanasieff, which provided the connection between the two singers (as did the record label, with Vandross also appearing on Columbia).

By the end of October, the single had reached its highest point, number 3 on the Hot 100. But by then there was word of a new Mariah Carey album, which had remained a well-kept secret in the trade until the middle of the month, when it was announced in *Billboard*.

The album, simply entitled *Merry Christmas*, appeared in record stores on November 1, heralded by a full-page advertisement in the Sunday *New York Times*. The timing, as intended, was perfect for the Christmas market, and showed that Columbia was quite definitely pitching Mariah as an entertainer, rather than limiting her to the pop market. Christmas albums have been part of the record business for many years, but as a general rule they're geared toward the mass (family) market, rather than the regular buyers of pop music (although Christmas singles traditionally do well on the pop charts). Christmas albums can be rereleased year after year, and as long as the performer remains popular, their sales tend to be consistent.

That would seem to further indicate that the label is looking at Mariah as a singer who'll be around for a long time. The album itself offers no evidence to the contrary, offering, essentially, something for everybody, from gospel and hymn to standards and pop.

Recorded at Sony Studios and the Hit Factory in New York, it utilizes many musicians who've worked with Mariah in the past. Needless to say, Walter Afanasieff plays a prominent role, coproducing and co-arranging the majority of the record's ten tracks, and playing keyboards. But Melanie Daniels, Shanrae Price, and Kelly Price also return to sing background vocals. Also introduced is a new face, Loris Holland, who co-arranges three tracks, and plays piano and Hammond organ on them—quite notably, the three most gospelish sounding songs on the disc.

For, finally, in this setting, Mariah's been able to record some real gospel music. Her version of "Silent Night" has large elements of the style, but it's on the final track. "Jesus, Oh What a Wonderful Child," a traditional song, that things really take flight. Sounding almost as if it could have been recorded in a church, a simple combo (keyboards, bass guitar, drums, some basic percussion, backing vocals, and Mariah) cut loose. Her love of the music truly comes through here, leading the band without pushing herself forward, letting the song develop and work out, trading lines with the chorus, until, after the crescendo, the musicians move into a fast double time to the end. As a finale to the album, it's perfect—pertinent to the season, uptempo, religious without being offensively so. And it does leave the listener wondering whether one day Mariah will indulge herself and record a whole album of gospel songs.

Most of the songs here are naturally very familiar. Her rendition of "Santa Claus Is Comin' to Town" might not be as rock'n'roll as the version Bruce Springsteen and the E Street Band released in 1981 (although it was recorded in 1975), but it's still sprightly and appealing, while Hoyt Axton's "Joy to the World," which was a number one hit for Three Dog Night in 1971, is joined with the traditional song of the same name to create something far less secular.

Mariah's never hidden her feelings about (and her gratitude to) God, although she's never pushed them on her audience, either. But the reverence in her heart is allowed to shine through in a gentle way on *Merry Christmas*. Half of the ten songs are religious, and quite unashamedly so, which is certainly appropriate, and perhaps even praiseworthy, as so much commerciality has taken over the season.

But there's still no danger of it becoming too serious, with tracks like "Santa Claus Is Comin' to Town" and a playful cover of "Christmas (Baby Please Come Home)," by the Spector/Barry/Greenwich team, which first saw light on Phil Spector's *Christmas Album* in 1963, sung by Darlene Love (also on that record, curiously, was the Ronettes' version of "Santa Claus Is Comin' to Town"). Mariah obviously loves the song, and while she and Walter Afanasieff don't try to reproduce Spector's trademark "wall of sound" technique, they have fun with the style.

Merry Christmas also contains three new Mariah Carey–Walter Afanasieff compositions. "All I Want for Christmas Is You," "Miss You Most (at Christmas Time)," and "Jesus Born on This Day." The first is uptempo, a love song that could quite easily have been written for Tommy Mottola, full of images of the Christmas magic that's all too often lost after childhood.

"Miss You Most (at Christmas Time)" is a sad ballad, very much in line with the work Mariah's produced in the past, the type of tune that's been a hit for her. Over keyboards and a synthesized orchestra, courtesy of Walter Afanasieff, Mariah sings of a long-gone lover, and crystallizes the way that Christmas brings memories of the past into focus.

But of these three songs, it's "Jesus Born on This Day" that's the most surprising. A full-blown production number, it utilizes not only Walter's synthesized orchestra, but background singers and a children's choir. The tune is quite solemn and hymn-like, but the arrangement, oddly, makes it less religious and rather more glitzy, behind lyrics that quite overtly praise Jesus.

As Mariah has stated, Christmas is her favorite time of the year, something for which she thanks her mother. So perhaps releasing a Christmas album comes as much from the season's joy as anything else—after all, she is in a position to do pretty much whatever she chooses. But at the same time—and this may be a happy coincidence—it fits in very, very well with the overall impression of Mariah as entertainer, a performer who can appeal to the moms and dads as much as the teenagers. Whether *Merry Christmas* will join the short list of classic Christmas records remains to be seen, and it'll be another ten or fifteen years before we know. But it's entirely possible. It has all the ingredients, some religious songs, some pop, some standards. And for those who appreciate her voice, best of all, it has Mariah Carey really singing gospel.

As she told Larry Flick in *CD Review*, "You have to have a nice balance between standard Christian hymns and fun songs. It was definitely a priority for me to write at least a few new songs, but for the most part people really want to hear the standards at Christmas, no matter how good a new song is."

But *Merry Christmas* certainly appeared set to do well in its first year, entering the Billboard chart at number 30 within two weeks of its release. The record label heavily pushed three of the tracks, aiming "Jesus Born on This day" at Christian and gospel stations, "Miss You Most (at Christmas Time)" at the urban contemporary market, and "All I want for Christmas Is You" at adult and Top 40 buyers, carefully segmenting to maximize the record's impact.

A video was also shot for "All I Want for Christmas Is You," showing Mariah romping in the snow, which premiered on MTV on November 28. However, all the filming was completed before the song was recorded, making the lip-synching a difficult process.

Then, to top everything off, a dance mix of "Joy to the World" was set for release.

But the star on the tree for the year came on December 14, with the Mariah Carey Christmas Special on MTV. In conjunction with the release of *Merry Christmas,* the music video channel had run a contest that offered a prize of a trip to New York, $10,000, and a chance to see Mariah and attend her December 8 concert for the Fresh Air Fund.

The one hour special, hosted by VJ Bill Bellamy, featured extensive footage of the winner, and also showed her spending some of her winnings. It also included the 'real' video for 'All I Want for Christmas Is You,' presented in a black-and-white '60s style, with gog-go dancers, backup singers, and Mariah herself, in a minidress, white boots and teased-up hair, looking like a member of the Ronettes.

The show climaxed with an out-and-out gospel performance of 'Joy to the World' from the benefit show. Helping underprivileged children has long been close to Mariah's heart—witness her other charity work—and this, combining that impulse with her singing, was a truly big-hearted gesture, which, with *Merry Christmas* climbing rapidly all the way to number 3, made a perfect cap for another marvellous year.

So THINGS look very bright for Mariah Carey. But it shouldn't be forgotten that she's also Mariah Mottola. Being the wife of the man who is arguably the world's most powerful record executive brings plenty of responsibilities, and, perhaps, even a few conflicts, when your husband is also the head of the label you record for.

There are functions to attend, hospitalities to be offered, whether one likes it or not. It's business, and marrying Tommy made her a part of it. With her he's undoubtedly romantic ("I was in London for a week," Mariah gushed happily, "and every morning he had two dozen pink roses sent to my room. By the end of the trip, it was filled with roses."), but at the office he's a hard-nosed, pragmatic businessman, whose time these days has to be occupied more than ever with work.

One of the more notable changes in 1995 is the way Mariah has begun dressing in public. The kid from Long Island who lived in one outfit for a year before getting her record contract has given way to the woman photographed (in leather, albeit all black) at the spring fashion shows in New York, or wearing a pastel suit designed by Karl Lagerfeld for Chanel. Suddenly she's become a dedicated follower of fashion. In many ways it was probably a necessity. After all, it wouldn't exactly be seemly for Mrs. Mottola to appear in public in leggings or jeans, whatever she might wear at home. It may well be that her interest in fashion has always existed, and she's only recently had the time and money to indulge it. However, her previous reliance on casual clothes make that unlikely. Instead, she's (at least publicly) conforming to the image that is expected of someone in her position.

She's also become more involved in charity work, primarily with the Police Athletic League in Manhattan, and others—in one instance combining it with this new love of fashion, as she attended a Chanel show and luncheon to benefit the obstetrics department of New York Hospital–Cornell Medical Center. While no one would reasonably doubt that such things are in her heart anyway, and she has said, "I try to be a good person and make a difference where I can, in the world and with people," once again, such involvement is expected of Mrs. Mottola. And by the end of the year, she'd become the spokeswoman for New York's Fresh Air Fund charity (for whom she performed the benefit concert on December 8), which changed the name of one of its camps, in Fishkill, New York, to Camp Mariah, in her honor.

That most of Mariah's charity work involves children is no real surprise. Her affinity for them is obvious, as is her naturalness with them, in her videos. And one day, almost certainly, she and Tommy will be parents themselves (he has two children from his previous marriage). And they have talked about it, although having babies remains on the back burner—as she's said before in interviews. But there is absolutely nothing to stop Mariah from being a mother and still enjoying her career; others have done it. And, since she is primarily a recording artist, it wouldn't even pose that many problems.

It has to be difficult for her at times, tempering her independence with her role as an executive's wife. Discussing business will certainly be a part of their daily routine, and Mariah's career is part of Tommy's business. She even admits that they "sometimes get in fights" about it, a perfectly natural state of affairs, given the circumstances.

Given her lack of interest in housekeeping, she's probably lucky to have married Tommy—"an incredible cook"—and to have plenty of money of her own. At least she can afford a housecleaner!

Her happiness—both with her marriage and what has happened in the rest of her life (and the two are intertwined in so many ways)—is evident in her frequent smiles. She's always had an optimistic, sunny attitude toward life, even when things were at their darkest, and now she has a real reason. "I'm really fortunate, I'm really happy, and I'm really lucky to be where I am," she announced.

With their upstate New York estate to escape to, and an apartment in Manhattan for time in town, they really can enjoy the very best of both worlds. The farm offers them both room to indulge their passions—animals, particularly horses, for Mariah, guns for Tommy—while the apartment gives them access to the hustle and bustle of the city, around which much of their lives must naturally revolve.

In all likelihood Mariah will keep the two aspects of her life separate; it would be almost impossible for her to do otherwise without some conflict of interest. There are people who feel that much of the attention lavished on her by the label is because she is the boss's wife (or girlfriend, as it was). That's a criticism she can't possibly answer, nor can he. In fact, the only possible response is to point to the sales figures and believe such words are only sour grapes. Success inevitably breeds jealousy and resentment, and all that can be done is to ignore it and go on. Time will tell its own tale.

So far Mariah has juggled her two selves very well, and it's hard to believe that will change. The first step, as they say, is the hardest, and Mariah has been striding out. Really, the future prospects for Mariah Carey are infinite. Indeed, they could be so heady that it's probably a good thing that her feet are so firmly planted on the ground—no superstar tantrums, no smashing of the paparazzi's cameras—and that's due in no small part to the way Patricia Carey brought her up. So far her life has moved so far and so fast that she's barely had time to enjoy it. "I don't even think about what I've achieved," she told Britain's *Q* magazine. "I haven't focused on it and I wish I had, because I really want to enjoy it, and I don't know if I *am* enjoying it, because I'm just going through my life like a bulldozer. I still haven't *marveled* at it."

But as she takes the time to look both forward and behind, she should be happy with what she sees, and she *should* marvel at it. The rapidly rising arc of her success has in itself been quite amazing. From her very first release she's been a star, and there are more high points in her brief career than most people in the business manage in a lifetime. It may seem to her that she's bulldozing her way through life, but to an outside observer it appears rather that she's skipping through it. She recognizes how lucky she's been, and she gives thanks where it's due—"I prayed very hard for this to happen and it happened." Her reputation is as squeaky clean as it's possible to be, which only goes to show her appeal as a role model—that it is possible to make it without resorting to insults, outrage, drugs, alcohol, or other kinds of sad behavior. She's never been fodder for the supermarket tabloids, probably to their great annoyance, since her picture on the cover would sell plenty of copies on a midweek morning.

Her fans (as well as those who don't care for her) have been able to trace her growth through her records—that being her main form of communication with the world. She's never been a critics' favorite. They've tended to see her as too packaged, too obvious in her appeal, and they've enjoyed taking her to task. But even the hardest-hearted among them couldn't deny her wonderful voice.

For all that, though, or perhaps because of it, she's never been featured in music magazines, although her vocal skill definitely qualifies her as a musician. Instead, it's the entertainment journalists who've picked up on her, the magazines like *People* and *Ebony*. And that kind of publicity, which ends up reaching a much larger readership, has labeled her a "personality," for better or worse.

In the long run, that turns out to be for the better. The interviews (if not the album reviews) have been flattering profiles, and have certainly helped her sell records and contributed toward making her something of an inspiration and even, perhaps, a bit of a music-business legend. She has, probably at the insistence of Columbia, been sparing in the number of interviews granted, which has meant that, unlike some others, she hasn't lived her entire life on magazine covers, even if, at times, it might have seemed so. Among her lesser-known awards are ones for "Sexiest Posture" from the American Chiropractic Association, a certificate proclaiming her one of the Top 100 Irish-Americans, and an accolade as one of *People* magazine's "50 Most Beautiful People" in 1991.

So far, as Mariah said, "I couldn't have made it any better if I'd created it myself," and that's quite true. Following her short tour she even seems to have accomplished the tremendous task of winning over the critics who'd readily panned her in the past—no small achievement in itself. Which leaves her able to make her next move with more or less a clean slate artistically. She'll be treated fairly by the press, which is about as much as anyone can ask, and she'll be able to bring to her next project a large amount of experience compressed into a few years.

If her releases so far have each shown great bounds forward, then a lengthy break should translate into a quantum leap stylistically. She'll still be writing popular songs, and not every single one will be a ballad (everyone needs some variety, and Mariah's still young enough to find the dance-music concept interesting)—although she's aware enough of her own strengths and weaknesses to know what works best for herself.

She (and a few others) have shown that it's possible to attain strong chart positions based on quality rather than image. Yes, Columbia's publicity campaign helped her break through initially, but it's been *her* songs and singing that have given her so many number 1 singles.

And it's not likely to all fall apart tomorrow. Unlike so many chart artists, her career isn't based on fad or fashion. She's not likely to go the way, say, of an MC Hammer or Vanilla Ice. She's found an audience, a large, consistent core who will continue to buy her records. As time goes by, the top singles may become fewer, but that's more or less par for the course. She's established now, a real force to be contended with, and now she can truly concentrate on her artistic growth—which is bound to be helped by the fact that she's contented in her home life. She'll continue to write inspirational lyrics, which is good, since so few people do it, and they'll continue to improve. Her music will become more sophisticated as she learns more, but it will probably always have that popular touch, that grounding in soul and gospel, music that moves a listener. And finally—even more than her very special voice—that's what will set her apart from other singers more than anything: her ability to write songs, to create for herself exactly what she wants to express. It gives her the edge, it makes everything more personal, more affecting. "All I can do now," she said, "is be the best I can be." She'll never stop trying, even when she could coast.

Mariah Carey is a remarkable woman; that's beyond any doubt. She gives herself to her music in a way most pop stars couldn't even imagine. It's impossible not to be at least a little in awe of her and her talent, and to wish her every success in the future, in everything she does.

CHRONOLOGY

1970
March 27   Mariah Carey born to Alfred Roy and Patricia
            Carey.

1972   Mariah's parents split up; divorce one year later.
            Mariah first demonstrates her singing talent correct-
            ing her mother.

1974   Patricia Carey begins giving her daughter singing
            lessons.

1976   Mariah makes her public singing debut.

1984   Mariah works part-time after school, singing on
            demo tapes at Long Island studios.

1986   For her sixteenth birthday, brother Morgan pays to
            make a professional 24-track demo in Manhattan.
            Here she meets Ben Margulies.

1987   Mariah graduates from Harborfields High School on
            Long Island. Patricia remarries. Mariah moves to
            Manhattan, keeps recording and pushing her tape to
            record companies.

1988   Mariah auditions and lands job singing backup for
            Brenda K. Starr.

November   Dragged by Brenda to a party, Mariah passes her
            tape to Columbia head Tommy Mottola. He listens
            to it in his limousine, turns around and searches for
            her. She has left. The following Monday he contacts
            her.

December   Mariah signs a contract with CBS Columbia.

1989   Spends the year recording her debut album with
            producers Narada Michael Walden, Ric Wake, and
            Rhett Lawrence, using a lot of the material she and
            Ben Margulies have written over the last three
            years.

1990

April
Mariah performs at an invitation-only Columbia party, accompanied by Richard Tee on piano. On the heels of this, she performs at the National Association of Recording Merchandisers convention in Los Angeles. After this comes a nine-city promotional tour, during which "Love Takes Time" is hastily recorded and added to the already completed album.

June
Mariah sings "America the Beautiful" before Game One of the NBA playoffs. This is followed by appearances on both "The Arsenio Hall Show" and "The Tonight Show."

June 2
"Vision of Love" enters the *Billboard* Hot 100 at number 73.

June 30
Mariah Carey debuts on the album chart at number 80.

August 4
"Vision of Love" reaches number 1. *Mariah Carey* starts a run of twenty-two weeks at the top of the album chart.

August 5
Mariah sings at the Camel Summer Jam in Mountain View, California.

October 27
Mariah is the musical guest on "Saturday Night Live."

November 10
"Love Takes Time" becomes Mariah's second number 1 single.

1991

February 20
Mariah wins two Grammys—for Best Pop Vocal Performance, Female, and Best New Artist—at the 33rd Annual Awards.

March 7
Mariah is named Best New Female Singer in the *Rolling Stone* Readers' Pick Music Awards.

March 9
"Someday" brings her string of number 1 singles to three.

March 12
At the "Soul Train" Awards, Mariah walks away with Best New R&B/Urban Contemporary Artist;

Best R&B/Urban Contemporary Single, Female; and Best R&B/Urban Contemporary Album, Female.

April 6   "I Don't Wanna Cry" enters the Hot 100 at number 50.

May 25   "I Don't Wanna Cry" hits number 1, making Mariah the first artist since the Jackson Five to have her first four singles top the chart.

Back in the studio, Mariah is working on her second album, with David Cole and Robert Clivilles, and Walter Afanasieff.

August 31   "Emotions," the title track and leadoff single from the new album, debuts at number 35.

October 12   "Emotions" reaches number 1, where it would stay for three weeks, making Mariah the first artist to have her first five singles go to that spot.

1992
January 25   "Can't Let Go," the second single from *Emotions,* peaks at number 2.

March 16   Mariah tapes MTV's "Unplugged" show.

May 28   "I'll Be There" enters the Hot 100 at number 13.

June 25   "I'll Be There" hits number 1, for the first of two weeks. At the same time, the *MTV Unplugged* EP enters the album chart at number 8. It would peak at number 3. Meanwhile, Mariah is involved with the writing and production of *Trey Lorenz,* then begins writing and recording her next album with a number of different partners, including Walter Afanasieff, the Cole-Clivilles team, and Babyface.

1993
June 5   Mariah and Tommy Mottola marry at St. Thomas Episcopal Church in New York. The reception is held at the Metropolitan Club, after which the couple honeymoons in Hawaii.

August 15   "Dreamlover" is released and enters the Hot 100 at number 13.

September 4	"Dreamlover" reaches number 1, where it will remain for eight weeks.
September 17	*Music Box* debuts on the album chart.
September 24	*Music Box* hits number 2. Tommy Mottola is promoted to President/COO, Sony Music.
November 3	Mariah's first tour begins at Miami Arena, Miami, Florida.
November 9	The tour continues at The Centrum, Worcester, Massachusetts.
November 17	On her sole Midwestern date, Mariah plays the Rosemont Horizon, Rosemont, Illinois.
November 25	The "Mariah Carey" television special airs on NBC.
December 2	With Trey Lorenz as supporting act, Mariah plays the Spectrum in Philadelphia.
December 10	The tour concludes at Madison Square Garden in New York.
December 25	"Hero" and *Music Box* both reach number 1 on their respective charts. *Music Box* will move up and down, but ends up spending a total of eight weeks in the top spot.

1994

January 31	"Without You" enters the Hot 100 at number 53.
March 25	"Without You" peaks at number 3.
May 20	"Anytime You Need a Friend" comes into the Hot 100 at number 45.
June 25	"Anytime You Need a Friend" stands at number 12.
November 1	*Merry Christmas* is released.
November 19	*Merry Christmas* enters the Billboard Album Chart at number 30.
December 8	Benefit concert for the Fresh Air Fund.
December 14	"Mariah Carey Christmas Special" airs on MTV.
December 25	*Merry Christmas* peaks at number 3, selling more than 3 million copies.

DISCOGRAPHY

Singles

Columbia 73348	"Vision of Love"	(1990)	#1
Columbia 73455	"Love Takes Time"	(1990)	#1
Columbia 73561	"Someday"	(1991)	#1
Columbia 73743	"I Don't Wanna Cry"	(1991)	#1
Columbia 73977	"Emotions"	(1991)	#1
Columbia 74088	"Can't Let Go"	(1991)	#2
Columbia 74239	"Make It Happen"	(1992)	#5
Columbia 74330	"I'll Be There"	(1992)	#1
Columbia 77080	"Dreamlover"	(1993)	#1
Columbia 77224	"Hero"	(1993)	#1
Columbia 77358	"Without You/Never Forget You"	(1994)	#3
Columbia 77528	"Anytime You Need a Friend"	(1994)	#12
Columbia 77629	"Endless Love" *(duet with Luther Vandross)*	(1994)	#3

Albums

Columbia CT45202	*Mariah Carey*	(1990)	#1
Columbia CT47980	*Emotions*	(1991)	#4
Columbia CT52758	*MTV Unplugged* EP	(1992)	#3
Columbia CT53205	*Music Box*	(1993)	#2
Columbia CT64222	*Merry Christmas*	(1994)	#3

Video Collections

SMV 19V-49072	*Mariah Carey—The First Vision*	(1991)
SMV 19V-49133	*Mariah Carey—"MTV Unplugged"* + 3	(1992)
SMV 19V-49179	*Mariah Carey*	(1993)

For those interested in contacting Mariah Carey,
or joining her fan club, the address is:

Mariah Carey Fan Club
P.O. Box 679
Branford, CT 06405